Get Started In Brazilian Portuguese

Sue Tyson-Ward and Ethel Pereira de Almeida Rowbotham

First published in Great Britain in 2015 by Hodder and Stoughton. An Hachette UK company.

British Library Cataloguing in Publication Data: a catalogue record for this title is available from the British Library.

Library of Congress Catalog Card Number: on file.

9781444198539

1

Cover image © Shutterstock

Typeset by Cenveo® Publisher Services.

Printed and bound in Great Britain by CPI Group (UK) Ltd., Croydon, CR0 4YY.

John Murray Learning policy is to use papers that are natural, renewable and recyclable products and made from wood grown in sustainable forests. The logging and manufacturing processes are expected to conform to the environmental regulations of the country of origin.

Carmelite House
50 Victoria Embankment
London EC4Y 0DZ
www.hodder.co.uk

Contents

About the authors

Sue Tyson-Ward has had a connection with Portuguese since living with a Portuguese family prior to starting her studies at Oxford in 1984. During her degree course she spent a year in Brazil, an experience which she has drawn on frequently over the years in her teaching and writing. Since graduating with a degree in Portuguese and Spanish in 1988, she has lived, worked and studied in Portugal, and has also been back to Brazil.

Sue has written a number of books on Portuguese and Brazilian language, life and culture. She was invited to act as language consultant for the BBC's highly acclaimed TV series *Talk Portuguese*, and also gave initial advice for the *Brazil Inside Out* series.

She has been involved in Portuguese examinations in the UK since 1992, including roles as Moderator for GCSE speaking tests, Principal Examiner for GCSE Writing and Principal Moderator for Asset Speaking tests; she was also the Subject Officer for Portuguese at the Awarding Body. She continues to act as a Vetter for International Examinations in Portuguese.

Sue teaches the language and culture in Lancaster, and prepares research students at the university for a variety of field trips to Brazil. She is a keen and enthusiastic promoter of all things relating to the Portuguese-speaking world.

Ethel Pereira de Almeida Rowbotham was born in Rio de Janeiro, moving later to Brasília, where she studied Politics and International Relations before moving to the UK. She has been teaching Portuguese at all levels in the UK for more than 20 years, and has worked at the University of Central Lancashire, Bolton Community College and Lancashire College, where she still teaches. She also works as an interpreter and translator and is a GCSE reviser.

How the book works

What you will learn identifies what you should be able to do in Portuguese by the end of the unit.

Culture points present cultural aspects related to the themes in the units, introducing key words and phrases and including follow-up questions.

Vocabulary builder introduces key unit vocabulary grouped by theme and conversation, accompanied by audio. By learning the words and listening to them, your progress in learning contemporary Brazilian Portuguese will be swift.

New expressions introduces the key expressions you will hear in the conversations. Listen to them on the audio and look at how they are expressed as these will aid your comprehension of the conversations. You will have the opportunity to use some of the expressions yourself in exercises and activities.

Conversations are recorded dialogues that you can listen to and practise, beginning with a narrative that helps you understand what you are going to hear, with a focusing question and follow-up activities.

Language discovery draws your attention to key language points in the conversations and to rules of grammar. Read the notes and look at the conversations to see how the language is used in practice.

Practice offers a variety of exercises, including speaking opportunities, to give you a chance to see and use words and phrases in their context.

Speaking and listening offer practice in speaking and understanding Portuguese through exercises that let you use what you have learned in previous units.

Reading and writing provide practice in reading everyday items and contain mostly vocabulary from the unit. Try to get the main point of the text before you answer the follow-up questions.

Pronunciation gives you another opportunity to focus on a particular tricky sound in Brazilian Portuguese, by listening to some words and imitating the native speaker.

Language tip boxes aim to give you extra snippets of vocabulary, cultural tips or helpful pointers for remembering specific expressions.

Test yourself helps you assess what you have learned. You learn more by doing the tests without consulting the text, and only when you have done them check if your answers are the correct ones (do not cheat!).

Self-check lets you see what you can do after having completed each unit.

To help you through the course, a system of icons indicates the actions to take:

 Listen to audio

 New words and phrases

 Speak Portuguese out loud

 Figure something out

 Culture tip

 Exercises coming up

 Reading passage

 Write and make notes

 Check your progress

Review units sum up what you have learned in the previous units. There are three review units: after Unit 3, after Unit 6 and after Unit 10. If you master all the questions in the review unit, go ahead with the next unit; if not, go back and refresh your knowledge.

The **Answer key** helps you check your progress by including answers to the activities both in the text units and the review units.

Once you have completed all ten units in this book successfully, you may want to proceed with more advanced Brazilian Portuguese course books, such as *Teach Yourself Complete Brazilian Portuguese*. Bilingual dictionaries and Portuguese grammars, such as the *Teach Yourself Essential Portuguese Grammar*, will be of much use. There are many internet resources for learning Portuguese, including sites for popular Brazilian journals, magazines and TV and radio stations.

Learn to learn

The Discovery method

This book incorporates the Discovery method of learning. You will be encouraged throughout the course to engage your mind and figure out the meaning for yourself, through identifying patterns and understanding grammatical concepts, noticing words that are similar to English, and more. As a result of your efforts, you will be able to retain what you have learned, use it with confidence and continue to learn the language on your own after you have finished this book.

Everyone can succeed in learning a language – the key is to know how to learn it. Learning is more than just reading or memorizing grammar and vocabulary. It is about being an active learner, learning in real contexts and using in different situations what you have learned. If you figure something out for yourself, you are more likely to understand it, and when you use what you have learned, you are more likely to remember it.

As many of the essential details, such as grammar rules, are introduced through the Discovery method, you will have more fun while learning. The language will soon start to make sense and you will be relying on your own intuition to construct original sentences independently, not just by listening and repeating.

Happy learning!

BE SUCCESSFUL AT LEARNING LANGUAGES

1 Make a habit out of learning

Study a little every day, between 20 and 30 minutes if possible, rather than two to three hours in one session. **Give yourself short-term goals**, e.g. work out how long you'll spend on a particular unit and work within the time limit. This will help you to **create a study habit**, much in the same way you would a sport or music. You will need to concentrate, so try to **create an environment conducive to learning** which is calm and quiet and free from distractions. As you study, do not worry about your mistakes or the things you can't remember or understand. Languages settle differently in our brains, but gradually the language will become clearer as your brain starts to make new connections. Just **give yourself enough time** and you will succeed.

2 Expand your language contact

As part of your study habit try to take other opportunities to expose yourself to the language. As well as using this book you could try listening to radio and television or reading articles and blogs. Perhaps you could find information in Brazilian Portuguese about a personal passion or hobby or even a news story that interests you. In time you'll find that your vocabulary and language recognition deepen and you'll become used to a range of writing and speaking styles.

3 Vocabulary

▶ To organize your study of vocabulary, group new words under:
   a generic categories, e.g. *food*, *furniture*.
   b situations in which they occur, e.g. under *restaurant* you can write *waiter*, *table*, *menu*, *bill*.
   c functions, e.g. greetings, parting, thanks, apologizing.
▶ Say the words out loud as you read them.
▶ Write the words over and over again. Remember that if you want to keep lists on your smartphone or tablet you can usually switch the keyboard language to make sure you are able to include all accents and special characters.
▶ Listen to the audio several times.
▶ Cover up the English side of the vocabulary list and see if you remember the meaning of the word.
▶ Associate the words with similar sounding words in English, e.g. **estudar** (*to study*) with the action of studying, **banco** with *bank*.
▶ Create flash cards, drawings and mind maps.
▶ Write words for objects around your house and stick them to the objects.
▶ Pay attention to patterns in words, e.g. adding **bom** or **boa** to the start of a phrase can often indicate a greeting, **bom dia**, **boa tarde**, **boa noite**.
▶ Experiment with words. Use the words that you learn in new contexts and find out if they are correct. For example, you learn in Unit 2 that **ter** means *to have*, e.g. **tenho dois filhos** (*I have two children / sons*), and is also used to say how old you are: **tenho 25 anos** (*I am 25 years old*). Experiment with **tenho** in new contexts, e.g. **tenho uma casa bonita** (*I have a pretty house*), **tenho um carro azul** (*I have a blue car*). Check the new phrases either in this book, in a dictionary or with Brazilian Portuguese speakers.

4 Grammar

▶ To organize the study of grammar write your own grammar glossary and add new information and examples as you go along.

- ▶ Experiment with grammar rules.
- ▶ Sit back and reflect on the rules you learn. See how they compare with your own language or other languages you may already speak. Try to find out some rules on your own and be ready to spot the exceptions. By doing this you'll remember the rules better and get a feel for the language.
- ▶ Try to find examples of grammar in conversations or other articles.
- ▶ Keep a 'pattern bank' that organizes examples that can be listed under the structures you've learned.
- ▶ Use old vocabulary to practise new grammar structures.
- ▶ When you learn a new verb form, write the conjugation of several different verbs you know that follow the same form.

5 Pronunciation

- ▶ When organizing the study of pronunciation keep a section of your notebook for pronunciation rules and practise those that trouble you.
- ▶ Repeat all of the conversations, line by line. Listen to yourself and try to mimic what you hear.
- ▶ Record yourself and compare yourself to a native speaker.
- ▶ Make a list of words that give you trouble and practise them.
- ▶ Study individual sounds, then full words.
- ▶ Don't forget, it's not just about pronouncing letters and words correctly, but also using the right intonation. So, when practising words and sentences, mimic the rising and falling intonation of native speakers.

6 Listening and reading

The conversations in this book include questions to help guide you in your understanding. But you can go further by following some of these tips.

- ▶ **Imagine the situation.** When listening to or reading the conversations, try to imagine where the scene is taking place and who the main characters are. Let your experience of the world help you guess the meaning of the conversation, e.g. if a conversation takes place in a snack bar you can predict the kind of vocabulary that is being used.
- ▶ **Concentrate on the main part.** When watching a foreign film you usually get the meaning of the whole story from a few individual shots. Understanding a foreign conversation or article is similar. Concentrate on the main parts to get the message and don't worry about individual words.
- ▶ **Guess the key words**; if you cannot, ask or look them up.
- ▶ When there are key words you don't understand, try to guess what they mean from the context. If you're listening to a Portuguese speaker

and cannot get the gist of a whole passage because of one word or phrase, try to repeat that word with a questioning tone; the speaker will probably paraphrase it, giving you the chance to understand it. If for example you wanted to find out the meaning of the word **molho** (*sauce*), you would ask **Que quer dizer molho?** or **O que é molho?**

7 Speaking

Rehearse in the foreign language. As all language teachers will assure you, the successful learners are those students who overcome their inhibitions and get into situations where they must speak, write and listen to the foreign language. Here are some useful tips to help you practise speaking Brazilian Portuguese:

▶ Hold a conversation with yourself, using the conversations of the units as models and the structures you have learned previously.

▶ After you have conducted a transaction with a sales assistant or waiter in your own language, pretend that you have to do it in Portuguese.

▶ Look at objects around you and try to name them in Portuguese.

▶ Look at people around you and try to describe them in detail.

▶ Try to answer all of the questions in the book out loud.

▶ Say the dialogues out loud then try to replace sentences with ones that are true for you.

▶ Try to role play different situations in the book.

8 Learn from your errors

▶ Don't let errors interfere with getting your message across. Making errors is part of any normal learning process, but some people get so worried that they won't say anything unless they are sure it is correct. This leads to a vicious circle as the less they say, the less practice they get and the more mistakes they make.

▶ Note the seriousness of errors. Many errors are not serious as they do not affect the meaning; for example if you use the wrong article (**o** for **a**) or the wrong pronouns (**ela fala** for **ele fala**). So concentrate on getting your message across and learn from your mistakes.

9 Learn to cope with uncertainty

▶ Don't over-use your dictionary. When reading a text in the foreign language, don't be tempted to look up every word you don't know. Underline the words you do not understand and read the passage several times, concentrating on trying to get the gist of the passage. If after the third time there are still words which prevent you from getting the general meaning of the passage, look them up in the dictionary.

▶ Don't panic if you don't understand.

▶ If at some point you feel you don't understand what you are told, don't panic or give up listening. Either try and guess what is being said and keep following the conversation or, if you cannot, isolate the expression or words you haven't understood and have them explained to you. The speaker might paraphrase them and the conversation will carry on.

▶ Keep talking.

▶ The best way to improve your fluency in the foreign language is to talk every time you have the opportunity to do so: keep the conversations flowing and don't worry about the mistakes. If you get stuck for a particular word, don't let the conversation stop; paraphrase or replace the unknown word with one you do know, even if you have to simplify what you want to say. As a last resort use the word from your own language and pronounce it in the foreign accent.

Brazilian Portuguese

Although Brazilian Portuguese is a 'variant' of the Portuguese language, just as that spoken in Portugal itself is, the Brazilians manage to make their language sound as laid-back as they are themselves. It is actually easier to understand a Brazilian speaker than a speaker of European Portuguese, as Brazilians tend to open their vowels more, so you can hear more of the words, and they often sound as though they are 'Samba-ing' round the language. Studded with all kinds of mannerisms and gestures, conversation with Brazilians is interesting, often fun, but sometimes needs time to work round some of the common speech habits. A typical example, often difficult to decipher for a foreigner listening in, is the contraction of the word **está** (*is / are*) to just **tá**. So, you may hear **tá legal!** (*that's great!*) – **legal** being one of those words used by every Brazilian to mean something is *great*, *super*, *wicked*, etc. Other such colourful expressions include: **beleza!** or **que beleza!** (*how fantastic!*), **ótimo** (*brilliant*), **tô (estou) nem aí** (*I'm not bothered*), **nossa!** (*wow!*), and **vij** (short for **Virgem Maria** – a more benign way of expressing 'God'-type phrases of amazement). Whoops of excitement are conveyed through **opa!** and **oba!**; anything in a mess or shambles is a **bagunça**, and if you are off to the beach, you may well be showing off your tanned **bum bum** in a **fio-dental** (*dental floss bikini*). Have fun!!

If you have had any previous exposure to the Portuguese spoken in Portugal, you will notice a few differences between that and Brazilian Portuguese, the main ones being the pronunciation of certain sounds and vocabulary. So, whereas in Portugal **boa noite** (*good evening*) is pronounced 'boh-uh noy-t', in Brazil you are more likely to hear 'boh-a noy-chee', the '-te' sound in Brazil being a distinctive '-chee'. In a similar way, the '-de' sound differs: the word for *city* (**cidade**) is usually 'see-da-duh' in Portugal, but 'see-da-dgee' in Brazil. There are slight regional variations, but on the whole the '-te' and '-de' sounds of Brazil are very easy to listen out for. In terms of vocabulary, in the same way as British and American English uses different words, so too do Brazilian and European Portuguese, sometimes to a confusing extent. A *train* is **comboio** in Portugal but **trem** in Brazil; *breakfast* in Portugal is **pequeno almoço** but **café da manhã** in Brazil. Some grammatical structures are also slightly different. The Portuguese, for example, will say **Chamo-me X** (*I am called X*), whereas a Brazilian would say **Eu me chamo X**; Brazilians call most people **Você** (*you*), but in Portugal there is a minefield of forms of address. Brazilians also incorporate many English words into their everyday speech, sometimes giving them their slant on pronunciation; the words **shopping** (*shopping centre*) and **short** (*shorts*) are commonplace.

Given the size of Brazil, Brazilian Portuguese has much more consistency as a language than many expect. Although not a lot of data exists as yet on the variations within Brazil, the main differences appear to be based on pronunciation, especially the vowel sounds. Some research to date has attempted to categorize a 'northern' and 'southern' group of variants. Some of the more distinct Brazilian Portuguese dialects include **Caipira**, generally considered a country dialect, spoken in many of the poorer and more rural areas mainly in the São Paulo state region; **Fluminense**, which is spoken in the state of Rio, while in the city of Rio both the dialect spoken and the inhabitants are known as **Carioca**; in Rio Grande do Sul, the **gaúcho** sound has been influenced by immigrants, mostly from Germany. There are also distinct dialects in the northern states of Ceará and Bahia. Of course, once you venture into the Amazon areas, you will encounter indigenous languages spoken by many indigenous tribes.

MAP OF BRAZIL

Pronunciation guide

Here is a simple guide to the letters of the alphabet, their Brazilian Portuguese name (in square brackets) and how to pronounce them.

The Portuguese alphabet is the same as the Roman one used in English and other Latin-based languages. Although the letters K, W and Y do not appear in native Brazilian words, the letters exist for use in foreign words and abbreviations, and under the new spelling agreement (see below) have been incorporated into the alphabet proper. Listen to the whole alphabet on the audio a few times, then try to join in.

 00.01

A [a] ah	**B** [bê] bay	**C** [cê] say	**D** [dê] day	**E** [é] eh	**F** [efe] eh-fee
G [gê] zhay	**H** [agá] ah-gah	**I** [i] ee	**J** [jota] zhoh-tah	**K** [ka] ka	**L** [ele] eh-lee
M [eme] eh-mee	**N** [ene] eh-nee	**O** [ó] oh	**P** [pê] pay	**Q** [quê] kay	**R** [erre] air-hee
S [esse] eh-ssee	**T** [tê] tay	**U** [u] oo	**V** [vê] vay	**W** [dáblio] dabble-yoo	**X** [xis] shish
Y [ípsilon] ip-see-lon	**Z** [zê] zay				

Most Portuguese words are pronounced as they are written – there are far fewer 'hidden' sounds or awkward sounds than in some other languages, such as English or French. However, when Brazilians speak, they often add a vowel, usually a **y** (ee) in words that end in some consonants (mainly **d**, **k**, **t**) such as:

Facebook (*Facybooky*)

Internet (*Internetchy*)

Ford (*Forjy*)

Fiat (*Fiatchy*)

Hot dog (*hotchy doggy*)

Names of people: *Mark* (*Marky*), *David* (*Davijy*), *Nick* (*Nicky*)

Portuguese also has its own version of many English words, such as:

picnic (**piquenique**)

whisky (**uísque**)

New York (**Nova Iorque**)

Once you have decoded a few tricky sounds, you should be able to have a go at reading Portuguese out loud as you see it. The following are some basic guidelines for some of the less straightforward pronunciations:

Portuguese letter(s)	Pronunciation
ch	*sh*
lh	like the *lli* in *million*
nh	like the *ni* in *onion*
g, followed by **e / i**	like the *s* in *pleasure*
j	as above
h	always silent
x	tricky – varies from a hard *ks* sound to a *z*, or even *sh*

Nasal sounds pronounced at the back of the nose are indicated by a ~ over the vowel, and also include words ending in **-m** or **-n**. Try to imagine saying them with a bad cold, when your nose is slightly blocked!

ão	*ow*
ãos	*ows*
õe	*oy*
ões	*oys*
ã	*ah*
ãs	*ahs*
ãe	*eye*
ães	*eyes*

One thing to remember is that when words run together when spoken, there is an effect on the ending and beginning of words involved, which may alter the sound from when a word is spoken in isolation from others.

A quick note here about the consonants **c**, **g** and **q**, which change their pronunciation depending on which vowels follow them. This can be a stumbling block for the uninitiated, hence a basic rule here:

c before **a**, **o** or **u** = hard sound, like *cat*

ç before **a**, **o** or **u** = soft sound, like *face*

c before **e** or **i** = soft sound

g before **e** or **i** = soft sound, like the *s* sound in *treasure*

g before **a**, **o** or **u** = hard sound, like in *goal*

g + u before **e** or **i** = 'silent' **u**, e.g. **guitarra** (*guitar*) = *ghee* … NOT *gwee* … There are some exceptions (there always are!), such as **linguiça** (*spicy sausage*) = *lingwiça*.

q is always followed by **u**

qu before **e** or **i** = 'silent' **u**, e.g., **máquina** (*machine*) *mákeena*, NOT *mákweena*; again, there are some exceptions – make a note of them when you learn them.

qu before **o** or **a** = *kw*, e.g. **quadro** (*picture*) = *kwadro*

ph does not exist in Portuguese: those words similar to English are spelled with an **f** – the sound is the same, but be careful with the spelling: e.g. **filósofo** (*philosopher*).

You will have the opportunity throughout the ten units of this course to focus on how to pronounce some of the trickier sounds. By listening carefully to the native speaker, and trying to imitate how they say the words, you will improve your spoken Portuguese enormously!

Brazilian spelling

After many years of wrangling over spelling throughout the Portuguese-speaking world (and most particularly between Portugal and Brazil), up-to-date orthographic (spelling) agreements are now being implemented under the new **Acordo Ortográfico**. However, there are still some differences in spelling between the two main variants of the language, Brazilian and Luso-African, which includes those African countries with Portuguese as an official language. If you have studied European Portuguese before now, you will notice slight differences in spelling, for example: EP **rececionista** / BP **recepcionista** (*receptionist*).

Accents

You will find the following written accents in Portuguese:

´	*acute accent*	**acento agudo**	opens vowel sound and indicates stress*	**cardápio** (*menu*)
^	*circumflex*	**circunflexo**	closes vowel sound and indicates stress	**inglês** (*English*)
~	*tilde*	**til**	nasalizes vowel and usually indicates stress	**estação** (*station*)

	grave accent	**acento grave**	opens vowel, non-stressing, indicates a contraction of two words	**àquela = a + aquela** (*to that*)

* Stress is when you emphasize part of a word, like the first syllable of the English word accent.

There are also the letter **ç c cedilha** (*c cedilla*), which makes the **c** soft, and the dieresis (two dots, like the German umlaut) to denote words of foreign origin in their original forms (e.g. **Müller**).

STRESS

Portuguese words are classified into three groups in terms of where the stress (emphasis) falls:

1 **last syllable**
2 **penultimate (next to last)**
3 **antepenultimate (third-last)**

The majority belong to Group 2 and do not usually require a written accent. The written accent occurs to enable words to be correctly stressed when they have deviated from the usual stress pattern. Whenever you see a written accent, that is where you should emphasize the word when you say it. Words also carry a written stress mark to distinguish them from a word with the same spelling but a different meaning, e.g. **por** (*by*) and **pôr** (*to put*). These are relatively rare.

A FEW TIPS TO HELP YOU ACQUIRE AN AUTHENTIC ACCENT

It is not absolutely vital to acquire a perfect accent – the aim is to be understood. Here are a number of techniques for working on your pronunciation:

1 Listen carefully to the audio or native speaker or teacher. Whenever possible repeat out loud, imagining you are a native Brazilian speaker of Portuguese.
2 Record yourself and compare your pronunciation with that of a native speaker.
3 Ask native speakers to listen to your pronunciation and tell you how to improve it.
4 Ask native speakers how a specific sound is formed. Watch them and practise at home in front of a mirror.
5 Make a list of words that give you pronunciation trouble and practise them.

Useful expressions

NUMBERS

 00.02

1	um / uma
2	dois
3	três
4	quatro
5	cinco
6	seis
7	sete
8	oito
9	nove
10	dez
11	onze
12	doze
13	treze
14	catorze
15	quinze
16	dezesseis
17	dezessete
18	dezoito
19	dezenove
20	vinte
21	vinte e um / uma
22	vinte e dois / duas
23	vinte e três
24	vinte e quarto
25	vinte e cinco

This pattern is maintained throughout all the tens, through to 99.

30	**trinta**	70	**setenta**
40	**quarenta**	80	**oitenta**
50	**cinquenta**	90	**noventa**
60	**sessenta**	100	**cem**
101	**cento e um, uma**	200	**duzentos / duzentas**
102	**cento e dois, duas**	300	**trezentos / trezentas**
125	**cento e vinte e cinco**	400	**quatrocentos / quatrocentas**
146	**cento e quarenta e seis**	500	**quinhentos / quinhentas**
163	**cento e sessenta e três**	600	**seiscentos / seiscentas**
178	**cento e setenta e oito**	700	**setecentos / setecentas**
182	**cento e oitenta e dois, duas**	800	**oitocentos / oitocentas**
199	**cento e noventa e nove**	900	**novecentos / novecentas**
1,000	**mil**		

DAYS OF THE WEEK

00.03

Sunday	**domingo**
Monday	**segunda-feira**
Tuesday	**terça-feira**
Wednesday	**quarta-feira**
Thursday	**quinta-feira**
Friday	**sexta-feira**
Saturday	**sábado**

MONTHS OF THE YEAR

January	**janeiro**
February	**fevereiro**
March	**março**
April	**abril**
May	**maio**
June	**junho**
July	**julho**
August	**agosto**

September	**setembro**
October	**outubro**
November	**novembro**
December	**dezembro**

EVERYDAY EXPRESSIONS

00.04

Can you repeat that, please?	**Pode repetir, por favor?**
Once more, please.	**Mais uma vez, por favor.**
Speak more slowly, please.	**Fale mais devagar, por favor.**
Do you understand?	**Você entende?**
I understand.	**Entendo.**
I don't understand.	**Não entendo.**
I don't know.	**Não sei.**
Is that correct?	**Está certo?**
That's right.	**Está certo. / Isso!**
Do you speak English?	**Você fala inglês?**
Do you speak Portuguese?	**Você fala português?**
I speak Portuguese, but not very well.	**Falo português, mas não muito bem.**
How much does it cost?	**Quanto custa?**
Where is …?	**Onde fica …? / Onde é …?**
I'm sorry!	**Desculpe!**
What time is it?	**Que horas são?**

GENERAL GREETINGS

Hi!	**Oi!**
Good morning. / Hello.	**Bom dia.**
Good afternoon. / Hello. (usually up to early evening)	**Boa tarde.**
Good evening. / Good night.	**Boa noite.**
Everything OK?	**Tudo bem?**
How are you?	**Como você está?**

I'm well. / I'm fine.	**Estou bem.**
Thank you. (said by a woman)	**Obrigada.**
Thank you. (said by a man)	**Obrigado.**
yes	**sim**
no	**não**
See you later.	**Até logo.**
See you tomorrow.	**Até amanhã.**
Goodbye.	**Adeus. / Tchau!**
Let's go!	**Vamos!**

BASIC QUESTIONS

How?	**Como?**
Who?	**Quem?**
When?	**Quando?**
Where?	**Onde?**
What… / Which…?	**Que… / O que…?**
Which (one / ones)?	**Qual? / Quais?**
Why…?	**Por que…?**
How much / How many?	**Quanto / Quanta / Quantos / Quantas?**

Como vai?

How are you?

In this unit, you will learn how to:
▶ *say* hello *and* goodbye.
▶ *introduce yourself and others.*
▶ *say where you come from and what languages*
  you speak.
▶ *say what your job or profession is.*
▶ *use the present tense of verbs.*
▶ *ask questions.*

CEFR: (A1) *Can establish basic social contact by using the simplest everyday polite forms of: greetings and farewells; introductions; Can ask and answer questions about themselves and other people.*

Brazil

O Brasil (*Brazil*) is the largest country in **América do Sul** (*South America*). It has borders with all the other South American countries, except with Chile and Ecuador. According to recent statistics, the Brazilian population is the sixth largest in the world. Brazil's rate of population growth has decreased dramatically in the last few decades due to the process of urbanization and modernization.

Brazil is divided into 26 **estados** (*states*) and one **Distrito Federal** (*Federal District*) where the capital, Brasília, is located. Most Brazilians live on or near the Atlantic coast of the **região Sudeste** (*South East region*) and of the **Nordeste** (*North East region*).

About 0.4 per cent of the total population are **índios** (*Indians*) – 57 per cent of them live in indigenous protected areas (12 per cent of the total territory of the country). Brazil has the largest number of people of Japanese ancestry outside Japan – most of them live in the state of São Paulo, along with large communities of **italianos** (*Italians*), **alemães** (*Germans*) and other European immigrants.

 Can you guess what the names of the other three regions of Brazil mean: **região Sul**, **região Norte** and **região Centro-Oeste**?

Vocabulary builder

01.01 Look at the words and phrases and complete the missing English expressions. Then listen and try to imitate the pronunciation of the speakers.

CUMPRIMENTOS	*GREETINGS*
Bom dia	*Good morning*
Boa tarde	*Good afternoon / Good evening*
Boa noite	_____ *evening* (later) */night*
Oi	*Hi / Hello*
Tudo bem? / Tudo bem	*Everything's OK? / Everything's fine*
Como está?	*How are you?* (more formal)
Como vai?	_____ *are you?* (less formal)
Muito prazer	*Pleased to meet you*
Até logo	*See you later / soon*
Até amanhã	*See you tomorrow*
Até mais tarde	_____ *later*
Tchau!	*Bye!*
Adeus	*Goodbye*

PERGUNTAS	*QUESTIONS*
Qual é o seu nome?	*What's your name?*
Como se chama?	*What are you called?*
Onde trabalha?	*Where do you work?*
O que faz?	*What (work) do you do?*
Qual é o seu email?	*What's your email?*
Você fala (espanhol)?	*Do you speak (Spanish)?*

NEW EXPRESSIONS

01.02 Look at the words and expressions that are used in the following conversation. Note their meanings.

Como está a senhora?	*How are you (madam)?*
Estou bem	*I'm well*
E o senhor, como vai?	*And you (sir), how are you?*
Obrigado/ obrigada	*Thank you (m/f)*
Desculpe	*Excuse me / I'm sorry*
Qual é o nome da senhora?	*What's your name?* (formal)
Chamo-me …	*I'm called …*
Trabalho por conta própria	*I work for myself*

(Eu) sou …	I am (I'm) …
Trabalho para …	I work for …
Que interessante!	How interesting!
Este é o meu colega	This is my colleague
Ele também é …	He is also a … / He's a … too
Ótimo!	Great! / Brilliant!
Então	Well then / So / In that case

Conversation 1

 01.03 *At a business meeting in Curitiba,* **senhor** *(Mr) Silva and* **senhora** *(Mrs) Costa chat during a coffee break.*

1 What is senhora Costa's first name?

Sr Silva	Bom dia. Como está a senhora?
Sra Costa	Bom dia. Estou bem, obrigada, e o senhor, como vai?
Sr Silva	Vou bem, obrigado. Desculpe, qual é o nome da senhora?
Sra Costa	Chamo-me Ana Costa. E o senhor?
Sr Silva	Paulo Silva. Onde a senhora trabalha?
Sra Costa	Trabalho por conta própria – sou advogada. E o senhor? O que faz?
Sr Silva	Eu sou engenheiro. Trabalho para Renault.
Sra Costa	Que interessante!
(Senhor Silva spots a colleague and introduces senhora Costa to him.)	
Sr Silva	Senhora Costa, este é o meu colega, José dos Santos. Ele também é engenheiro.
Sra Costa	Muito prazer!
Sr Silva	Ótimo! Então, até mais tarde.
Sra Costa	Até logo!

2 Read the conversation again, and with the help of the new expressions, answer the questions.
   a What time of day does the conversation take place?
   b What is senhora Costa's profession?
   c What is the name of senhor Silva's colleague?

3 Answer true or false to the following statements.
   a Senhora Costa works for herself.
   b Senhor Silva is a lawyer.
   c Senhora Costa says *See you tomorrow*.

4 Now listen to the conversation again, repeating after each line, and concentrating on your pronunciation.

> ### LANGUAGE TIP
> To call someone *you* in Brazil, use **o senhor** for men, and **a senhora** for ladies, in situations requiring formality and polite exchange, such as with strangers and in business meetings; **senhor** and **senhora** also mean *Mr* and *Mrs*. You will hear most Brazilians call each other **você** for *you*, which is less formal.
> Many Brazilians say **Eu me chamo X**, instead of **Chamo-me X**.

Language discovery 1

1 Identify the words for *I* and *he* in these expressions from the conversation:

a Eu sou engenheiro (*I am an engineer*)
b Ele é engenheiro (*He is an engineer*)

2 Which Portuguese words translate the verb *I am* in the following expressions?

a estou bem
b sou engenheiro

3 Look at these expressions from the conversation, and decide why the words in bold change in form:

a Como **está** a senhora? (*How are you?*)
b **Estou** bem, obrigada. (*I'm well, thank you*)

1 PERSONAL (SUBJECT) PRONOUNS

In Portuguese, the words for *I*, *you*, *he*, etc., also called subject pronouns, are not always needed, as the ending of the verbs (action words) indicates who is carrying out the action. They are needed, however, to avoid ambiguity, when some verb forms are identical, and they can also be used for emphasis. Here are the subject pronouns you will use in Brazilian Portuguese:

eu	*I*	**nós**	*we*
você[1]	*you* (singular)	**vocês**[1]	*you* (plural)
ele / ela	*he / she / it*[2]	**eles**[3] **/ elas**	*they*

[1] use **o senhor / a senhora** and the plurals **os senhores / as senhoras** in formal situations, but follow the same verb endings as for **você / vocês**

[2] both **ele** and **ela** are used to mean *it*, depending on the gender of the word in question

[3] **eles** is used for groups of two or more males and mixed groups of males and females

2 THE VERB *TO BE* – **SER**

Portuguese has two verbs meaning *to be*: **ser** and **estar**. **Ser** is used for permanent characteristics; use it to give your profession, or nationality.

eu sou	*I am*	nós somos	*we are*
você é	*you are* (sing)	vocês são	*you are* (pl)
ele / ela é	*he / she / it is*	eles / elas são	*they are*

PROFISSÕES E COMÉRCIOS

masculine	feminine	
médico	médica	*doctor*
professor	professora	*teacher*
gerente	gerente	*manager*
empregado	empregada	*employee / clerk / maid* (f)
encanador	encanadora	*plumber*
eletricista	eletricista	*electrician*
cozinheiro	cozinheira	*cook*

You don't need to say the word for *a* before your profession in Portuguese; simply state, for example, *I am teacher*.

3 THE VERB *TO BE* – **ESTAR**

Estar is used for situations of a more temporary nature; use it to ask how someone is or to enquire where someone is.

eu estou	nós estamos
você está	vocês estão
ele / ela está	eles / elas estão

Here are some interesting uses of the verb **estar**:

estar com fome	*to be hungry*
estar com frio	*to be cold* (person)
estar com calor	*to be hot* (person)
estar com pressa	*to be in a hurry*
estar com sede	*to be thirsty*

These literally mean *to be with hunger, with cold*, etc.

Practice 1

1 Complete each sentence using one of the words from the box.

eu você nós ele

a _____ está bem?

b Este é José; _____ é encanador.

c _____ sou professor.

d _____ estamos bem.

2 Complete the missing words.

	masculine	feminine	English
a	**médico**	_____	*doctor*
b	**professor**	**professora**	_____
c	_____	**gerente**	*manager*
d	**enfermeiro**	_____	*nurse*
e	_____	**eletricista**	*electrician*

3 Choose the correct verb (ser or estar) for each sentence.

a Como é / está o senhor?

b Sou / Estou advogado.

c Estou / Sou bem, obrigada.

d Ela também é / está secretária (*secretary*).

4 Match the Portuguese and English.

a Nós estamos com fome.   **1** Are you in a hurry?

b Ela está com calor?   **2** I am thirsty.

c Você está com pressa?   **3** We are hungry.

d Eu estou com sede.   **4** Is she hot?

5 01.04 Listen for people's nationalities and their professions.

	Nacionalidade	O que faz?
a Ana	_____	_____
b Peter	_____	_____
c Isabel	_____	_____
d Paulo	_____	_____

6 01.05 Listen and fill in the gaps with the missing words.

a Meu _____ é João Mendes da Silva.

b Sou _____ São Paulo, mas _____ em Brasília.

c _____ dentista e trabalho por conta _____.

d Sou recepcionista; _____ Mônica.

e Ela _____ portuguesa.

7 **01.06** **What is the matter with each person? Circle the correct answer.**

a Carlos is	thirsty	in a hurry	cold
b Joaquim is	hot	hungry	thirsty
c Anita is	cold	hungry	in a hurry
d Catarina is	hot	thirsty	in a hurry

Conversation 2

 01.07 Some international research students exchange information about themselves at their first seminar.

Read and listen to the conversation, then answer the questions.

1 What languages does Bruno speak?

Ornella	Oi, tudo bem?
Bruno	Tudo bem. Qual é o seu nome?
Ornella	Eu sou Ornella. E você?
Bruno	Meu nome é Bruno. De onde você é, Ornella?
Ornella	Eu sou italiana, de Roma. E você?
Bruno	Sou francês, de Toulouse.
Ornella	Você fala inglês?
Bruno	Falo, sim – inglês e também espanhol. E você?
Ornella	Bem, falo inglês e alemão.
Bruno	Ornella, você está no Facebook?
Ornella	Não, não estou.
Bruno	Então, qual é o número do seu celular?
Ornella	É 0797-33314558

(Bruno spots his friend, Mônica, approaching, and introduces Ornella to her.)

Bruno	Ah, Ornella, esta é a minha amiga, Mônica – ela é argentina.
Ornella	Tudo bem Mônica?

2 Read the conversation again and choose the correct answer to the questions.

a	What nationality is Ornella?	Spanish / Italian
b	Which city is Bruno from?	Rome / Toulouse
c	Which languages does Ornella speak?	English and French / English and German

d Is Ornella on Facebook?	Yes / No
e Whose phone number is 0797-33314558?	Bruno's / Ornella's
f Where is Mônica from?	USA / Argentina

 **Language discovery 2**

1 Find the expressions in the conversation which mean:
   a Do you speak English?
   b I speak English

2 In the conversation, Bruno says Sou francês … falo … inglês (*I am French … I speak … English*)**. What do you think it would mean if someone were to say Sou inglês … falo francês?**

> You may not always hear the little words **o** and **a** in the expressions **o meu, o seu, a minha**, and so on; some Brazilians don't include them at all.

1 PRESENT TENSE OF VERBS ENDING IN -AR

The present tense of verbs is used to describe actions you carry out regularly or which are a statement of fact. Look at how it works with a verb ending in -ar.

Remove the **-ar** then add the following endings:

falar *to speak*			
eu	**fal + o = falo** *I speak*	**nós**	**fal + amos = falamos** *we speak*
você	**fal + a = fala** *you speak* (sing)	**vocês**	**fal + am = falam** *you speak* (pl)
ele / ela	**fal + a = fala** *he / she / it speaks*	**eles / elas**	**fal+am = falam** *they speak*

To make a verb negative, put the word **não** before it

não falo inglês   *I don't speak English*

To make a question with the verb, simply lift up the intonation of your voice at the end of the sentence to make it sound like a question. Portuguese does not translate the equivalent of the English *do …?* or *does …?*

| **não** | *no / not* |
| **sim** | *yes* |

2 LANGUAGES AND NATIONALITIES

The language of a country is the same word in Portuguese as the masculine form of the nationality. When talking about the nationality of women, you need to use the feminine version of the word. Look at these examples and keep an eye out for similar patterns:

language	masculine nationality	feminine nationality	
italiano	italiano	italiana	*Italian*
inglês	inglês	inglesa	*English*
espanhol	espanhol	espanhola	*Spanish*
alemão	alemão	alemã	*German*

Falo um pouco de italiano.	*I speak a bit of Italian.*
Falo francês bem.	*I speak French well.*
Não falo inglês muito bem.	*I don't speak English very well.*

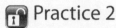 Practice 2

1 Add the correct verb endings.

a Eu fal _____ inglês.

b Elas não fal _____ francês.

c O senhor fal _____ português?

d Nós não fal _____ grego (*Greek*).

2 Make the sentences negative.

a Você é de Londres (*London*).

b Meu nome é Marcos.

c Paulo fala alemão.

d Ela é americana (*American*).

3 Complete the words of nationality.

a __t__li__na

b al__ __ã__

c f__ __nc__s

d es__an__ol__

 4 Translate the following sentences and then say them out loud in Portuguese.

a I speak a bit of Portuguese.

b I don't speak Greek.

c We speak French well.

Reading

Pedro introduces himself:

> Olá! Sou Pedro Rodrigues de Carvalho. Sou brasileiro, de Campinas, mas (*but*) agora moro (*I live*) em São José dos Campos. Sou engenheiro mecânico e trabalho na EMBRAER. Falo um pouco de espanhol e um pouco de inglês. Este é o meu amigo Eduardo Watanabe. Ele também trabalha na EMBRAER.

According to the text, are these statements true or false?

- **a** Pedro was born in São José dos Campos.
- **b** Pedro speaks English fluently.
- **c** Pedro is an engineer.
- **d** His friend does not work at EMBRAER.

 # Reading and writing

> Sou de Uberlândia, mas agora moro em Belo Horizonte.
> *I am from Uberlândia, but now I live in Belo Horizonte.*

Using this sentence as a model, fill in the gaps in the following sentences with the words that are missing. Then try to create sentences by following the instructions.

- **a** Sou de Recife, mas _____ moro _____ Salvador.
- **b** Sou _____ Belém, _____ agora moro em Fortaleza.
- **c** _____ de Ubatuba, mas agora _____ em São Paulo.
- **d** Translate: *I am from Brasília, but now I live in London.*

  _____

- **e** Create a sentence yourself, following the same pattern.

  _____

 # Speaking

1 Try to answer these questions in Portuguese.

- **a** Você é americano(a)?
- **b** Você fala inglês?
- **c** O Roberto é de São Paulo?
- **d** Onde você mora?
- **e** A Cristina é sua amiga?

2 **01.08** **Pronunciation practice**

The following words from the conversations all had the letter combination **nh** in them: **senhor**, **senhora**, **engenheiro**, **espanhol**, **cozinheira**. It sounds like the *ni* sound in the English word *onion*. Listen to them again now and repeat them, concentrating hard on sounding like the native speaker.

Go further

In Brazil, people tend to have two or more **sobrenomes** (*surnames*), at least one from the mother and one from the father – for example **Sônia Macedo da Silva**. When a woman gets married, she can add her husband's surname at the end, becoming **Sônia Macedo da Silva Costa** – **Macedo** from the mother, **da Silva** from the father and **Costa** from her husband; or she can remove the mother's name (**Macedo**, in this case) and add the husband's name (becoming **Sônia da Silva Costa**) to make it shorter, or she can keep her name as it is and not add the husband's surname at all. Looking at the telephone book you will see that many Brazilians have foreign surnames – German, Italian, Polish, Japanese – reflecting the origin of their grandparents or great-grandparents. Some have unusual first names, made up by the parents, including foreign names written as they sound to them in Portuguese, such as **Uoshinton**, **Maicon**, **Madenusa**, **Djenifer** and other creations. When discussing people using first names, it is common to insert **o** before male names, and **a** before female names, such as **o Pedro** and **a Ana**, although not all Brazilians do this.

 Test yourself

1 Match each question on the left to the corresponding correct answer on the right.

a Como se chama?	**1** Trabalho por conta própria.
b Onde trabalha?	**2** É pedro.paulo@hotmail.com
c O que faz?	**3** Sim, falo um pouco de alemão.
d Qual é o seu email?	**4** Chamo-me Alberto.
e Você fala alemão?	**5** Sou professor.

2 Fill the gaps to complete the sentences.

   a Bom _____. _____ vai?
   b _____ é meu colega.
   c Oi, _____ bem?
   d _____ prazer!

3 Make the sentences plural.

   a Eu falo inglês.
   b Ela não fala português.
   c Você fala grego?

SELF CHECK

I CAN ...
... say *hello* and *goodbye*.
... introduce myself and others.
... say where I come from and what languages I speak.
... say what my job or profession is.
... use the present tense of verbs.
... ask questions.

2 Você é casado?

Are you married?

In this unit, you will learn how to:
▶ *talk about how old people are.*
▶ *talk about your family.*
▶ *express marital status.*
▶ *use numbers from 0 to 100.*
▶ *describe people.*
▶ *discuss where people are studying.*

CEFR: (A1) *Can handle numbers; can ask and answer questions about themselves and other people;* **(A2)** *Can describe his / her family.*

Os brasileiros

Brazilians are very sociable and family-oriented. They like to speak about themselves and their **famílias** (*families*) and are very interested in getting to know people from other parts of the **país** (*country*) and of the **mundo** (*world*). They will be curious to know if you are **solteiro** (*single*) or **casado** (*married*), if you have children, where you live, what you do for a living and other information that you may consider intrusive, but they just want to get to know you and perhaps make a new **amigo** (*friend*). Very few Brazilians can speak English fluently – most can speak only a few words or sentences – so you will need to speak Portuguese if you want to make the most of your stay in Brazil.

Many Brazilians are **funcionários públicos** (*civil servants*) as those jobs tend to be more stable and secure. Selection for these jobs is made at national, state and municipal levels through an exam known as the **concurso público**, designed according to each position – some will require a university degree, others secondary school or primary school level. Post office workers, teachers in state schools and universities, policemen and judges all have to pass a similar exam.

At the end of the **ensino médio** (*secondary school*) the students sit a national exam called **ENEM** and depending on their final score they can enter the **universidade** (*university*) of their choice – or not.

Can you guess what João is saying about himself? **Sou solteiro, sou funcionário público e não falo inglês.**

Vocabulary builder

 02.01 Look at the words and phrases and complete the missing English expressions. Then listen and try to imitate the pronunciation of the speakers.

A FAMÍLIA	*THE FAMILY*
o marido/o esposo	*husband*
a mulher/a esposa	*wife*
o namorado	*boyfriend*
a namorada	_____
o filho	*son*
a filha	_____
o irmão	*brother*
a irmã	_____
o pai	*father*
a mãe	*mother*

 NEW EXPRESSIONS

 02.02 Look at the words and expressions that are used in the following conversation. Note their meanings.

Você é casado?	*Are you married?*
Qual é o nome dela?	*What's her name?*
Tenho uma foto dela	*I have a photo of her*
Ela é muito bonita!	*She is very pretty!*
Ela é linda mesmo!	*She's really gorgeous!*
Você tem filhos?	*Do you have (any) children?*
um filho só	*one son only / just one son*
Quantos anos ele tem?	*How old is he? (lit. How many years does he have?)*
… está no segundo ano de Direito	*… is in the second year of Law*
… quer ser advogado	*… wants to be a lawyer*
… é mais velho	*… is older*
tem o seu próprio negócio	*he has his own business*
ele vende peças de automóveis	*he sells motor car parts*
Ah é?	*Really? / Is that so?*
aqui vem	*here comes*
Oi querida! Então?	*Hi darling! Well then?*

Conversation 1

 02.03 *Rosa and Fernando are waiting for their partners after a meeting; they chat about their families.*

1 What is Fernando's girlfriend called?

Rosa	Então, Fernando, você é casado?
Fernando	Casado, não; sou separado, mas tenho uma namorada.
Rosa	Qual é o nome dela?
Fernando	Ela se chama Luciana. Tenho uma foto dela aqui no celular.
Rosa	Ela é muito bonita!
Fernando	Ela é linda mesmo!
Rosa	Você tem filhos, Fernando?
Fernando	Tenho, sim – um filho só.
Rosa	Quantos anos ele tem?
Fernando	O Felipe tem dezenove anos, está no segundo ano de Direito; quer ser advogado.
Rosa	Eu tenho uma filha que também é estudante. O meu filho, Marcelo, é mais velho; tem o seu próprio negócio; ele vende peças de automóveis.
Fernando	Ah é?
(Rosa sees her husband approaching.)	
Rosa	Ah, aqui vem o meu marido. Paulo, estamos aqui!
Paulo	Oi querida! Então?
Rosa	Paulo, este é o Fernando. Ele trabalha para o Banco do Brasil.
Paulo	Muito prazer.

2 Read the conversation again and, with the help of the new expressions, answer the questions.

    a Does Fernando have any children?
    b Who is 19 years old?
    c Who is Paulo?

 3 Now listen to the conversation again, repeating after each line and concentrating on your pronunciation.

> **LANGUAGE TIP**
>
> The plural of **filho** (*son*), **filhos**, can mean *sons* or *sons and daughters*; **pais** means *parents*, and **irmãos** means either *brothers* or *brothers and sisters*.
> To express marital status, use: **casado** (*married*), **divorciado** (*divorced*), **solteiro** (*single*), **separado** (*separated*) or **viúvo** (*widowed*). Change the final **-o** of each word to an **-a** to describe a woman's status.

💡 Language discovery 1

1 **Identify the Portuguese verb for** *I have* **in the following expression:**

tenho uma namorada   tenho uma foto

2 **Which Portuguese word means** *he sells* **in the following expression?**

…vende peças de automóveis.

3 **Which two words in the conversation mean** *a*, **as in** *a son and a daughter*, **and why do you think there are two versions of the word in Portuguese?**

1 THE VERB *TO HAVE* – TER

The Portuguese verb *to have*, **ter**, is formed as follows:

eu tenho	*I have*	**nós temos**	*we have*
você (etc.) **tem**	*you have* (singular)	**vocês têm**	*you have* (plural)
ele / ela tem	*he / she / it has*	**eles / elas têm**	*they have*

This is the everyday verb to express what you have or do not have. For example, *I have a son; I have a photo.*

> **LANGUAGE TIP**
>
> The verb **ter** is also used in the expression for talking about age. **Quantos anos você tem?** *How old are you?* (lit. *How many years do you have?*) **Tenho XX anos.** *I am XX.* (lit. *I have XX years.*)

2 A REGULAR -ER ENDING VERB – PRESENT TENSE

Many regular verbs in Portuguese fall into the group ending in **-er**, which are formed as follows: first, remove the **-er**, then add endings to what is left (known as the stem) to denote who is carrying out the action.

Look at the verb *to sell*, **vender**:

vender – er = vend (stem)			
eu vendo	*I sell*	**nós vendemos**	*we sell*
você vende	*you sell*	**vocês vendem**	*you sell*
ele / ela vende	*he / she / it sells*	**eles / elas vendem**	*they sell*

3 HOW TO TRANSLATE *A / AN* AND *THE*

The Portuguese words for *a / an* and *the* have to match the item they are with in terms of whether they are masculine or feminine, and singular or plural:

	masculine	feminine	masculine plural	feminine plural
a / an, some	**um**	**uma**	**uns***	**umas***
the	**o**	**a**	**os**	**as**

*the plurals **uns** and **umas** are sometimes replaced by the alternative words for *some*, **alguns** and **algumas**. In other situations, they are often just omitted.

A brother is **um irmão**, *the daughters* **as filhas**. As you go along, make sure you learn whether each noun (word for a thing, person or concept) is masculine or feminine by checking in the word lists or a dictionary.

NUMBERS 0–100

You may need to refresh your memory on number formation by looking back to the introductory material of this course and listening to the numbers on the audio. Here are some sample numbers to help you. Look at the patterns of formation to help you remember them:

0 **zero**	4 **quatro**	8 **oito**
1 **um**	5 **cinco**	9 **nove**
2 **dois***	6 **seis**	10 **dez**
3 **três**	7 **sete**	

11 **onze**	15 **quinze**	19 **dezenove**
12 **doze**	16 **dezesseis**	20 **vinte**
13 **treze**	17 **dezessete**	
14 **catorze**	18 **dezoito**	

21 **vinte e um**	58 **cinquenta e oito**	83 **oitenta e três**
34 **trinta e quatro**	60 **sessenta**	95 **noventa e cinco**
46 **quarenta e seis**	72 **setenta e dois**	100 **cem**

*the number two has a masculine form (**dois**) and a feminine (**duas**). Use the masculine form for normal counting, money and years; use the feminine version when referring to anything feminine, e.g., **duas filhas** *two daughters*.

primeiro	*first*
segundo	*second*
terceiro	*third*

 ## Practice 1

1 Complete each sentence by choosing the correct part of the verb ter.

- **a** Quantos anos você tem / têm ?
- **b** Eu tenho / tem 19 anos.
- **c** Nós têm / temos seis primos (*cousins*).
- **d** O José tem / tenho o seu próprio negócio.

2 Correctly form the verbs to complete the sentences.

  a (vender *to sell*)   Ela _____ produtos de limpeza (*cleaning products*).

  b (comer *to eat*)   Eu _____ bananas.

  c (beber *to drink*)   Vocês _____ café (*coffee*)?

  d (escrever *to write*)   Nós _____ uma carta (*a letter*).

  e (correr *to run*)   O Roberto _____ na praia (*on the beach*).

3 Make the statements singular. Follow the example.

  as irmãs ⟶ a irmã

  a uns (alguns) filhos ⟶ _____

  b umas (algumas) namoradas ⟶ _____

  c os advogados ⟶ _____

  d as mães ⟶ _____

4 Complete the number sequences.

  a três, quatro, cinco, _____, _____

  b vinte e nove, vinte e oito, _____, vinte e seis

  c _____, noventa e quatro, noventa e seis

  d quarenta, cinquenta, _____, setenta, _____

  e quinze, vinte, vinte e cinco, _____, _____

5 02.04 Now listen to Fábio speaking about himself and his family. Then answer the questions.

nós dois	*both of us*
Universidade Federal	*Federal University*

  a How old is Fábio?

  b What is he studying at university?

  c How old is his sister Heloísa?

  d What does their mother do?

Conversation 2

 02.05 *Three friends, Mateus, Simone and Helena, are looking at family photos on Facebook.*

Read and listen to the conversation, then answer the questions.

1 How old is Gilberto?

Mateus	Olha gente! Aqui tem uma foto da minha mãe!
Simone	Ela é muito bonita! O que ela faz?
Mateus	Ela é dona de casa. Ah, este é o meu irmão mais velho, o Gilberto.
Helena	Nossa, que gato!
Mateus	Ele é lindo mesmo! Ele é alto e moreno, e tem os olhos azuis.
Helena	Quantos anos ele tem?
Mateus	O Gilberto tem vinte e dois anos – ele faz anos em abril.
Helena	Onde ele estuda?
Mateus	Está na faculdade de Medicina – primeiro ano.
Helena	Ah é? Interessante!
Mateus	E você, Simone, também tem fotos?
Simone	Tenho, sim. Gente, estes são os meus pais, e esta é a minha irmã mais nova, a Tânia.
Mateus	É estudante?
Simone	Não. Ela é recepcionista no Hotel Ipanema.

2 Read the conversation again and answer the statements with True or False.

a Mateus' mother is a housewife. _____

b Gilberto's birthday is in April. _____

c Gilberto is in the third year of Medicine. _____

d Simone's sister is called Helena. _____

e Simone's sister works in a hotel. _____

AUTHENTIC EXPRESSIONS

Nossa!	*Wow!*
Gente!	*Folks! / Gang! / You guys!*
Olha gente! / Olhe gente!	*Look, gang! / Look here!*
Que gato / gata!	*He's / She's really gorgeous! (lit. What a cat!)*
Que lindo!	*He's so handsome! / It's so pretty!*

> ### DESCRIBING EYES
> **tem os olhos ... azuis / verdes /**   *he / she has blue /green /*
>   **pretos / castanhos**   *dark (black)/brown eyes*

> ### DESCRIBING HAIR COLOUR
> **tem os cabelos** *(hair)* **pretos /**   *he / she has black / brown / blonde / red hair*
>   **castanhos / loiros / ruivos** OR
>   **tem o cabelo preto / castanho**
>   **/ loiro / ruivo**

> ### DESCRIBING PEOPLE
> **alto**   *tall*
> **baixo**   *short*
> **moreno**   *tanned*
> Change the final **-o** to **-a** to describe a woman.

Language discovery 2

1 **Which word for** *pretty* **is used to describe Mateus' mother?**

2 **In the conversation, find the Portuguese expressions for** *older* **and** *younger.*

3 **Look at this expression from the conversation: O Gilberto tem vinte e dois anos – ele faz anos em abril. It means** *Gilberto is 22 (years old)* **– ... Can you work out how to translate the rest?**

4 **Why do you think there is a difference between the expressions for** *my* **in the following:**

o meu irmão *(my brother)*   **os meus pais** *(my parents)*

1 ADJECTIVES (DESCRIBING WORDS)

Words which describe (adjectives), such as *tall, short, old, young*, etc., change their ending in Portuguese to match what they are describing in terms of whether the thing or person is masculine, feminine, singular or plural. Most regular Portuguese adjectives end in **-o**, and form their changes like this:

	masc. sing.	fem. sing.	masc. pl.	fem.pl
alto *(tall)*	alto	alta	altos	altas

2 COMPARATIVES: EXPRESSING *OLDER, YOUNGER, WISER*, ETC.

To say something is *older, younger, prettier*, etc., in Portuguese you use the word for *more* (**mais**), with the appropriate adjective, remembering to change its ending if necessary.

ela é mais bonita *she is prettier*

vocês são mais velhos *you are older*

Note the following word order: **a Sandra é a minha irmã mais velha** *Sandra is my older sister* (lit. *Sandra is my sister more old*). The word used for *young*, **novo**, actually means *new*.

3 THE VERB *TO DO / TO MAKE* – FAZER

The Portuguese verb **fazer** means *to do* or *to make*. It is widely used, so now's a good time to learn it.

eu faço	*I do / make*	**nós fazemos**	*we do / make*
você (etc.) **faz**	*you do / make* (singular)	**vocês fazem**	*you do / make* (plural)
ele / ela faz	*he / she / it does / makes*	**eles / elas fazem**	*they do / make*

> Use **fazer** to say when your birthday is: **faço anos em setembro** *it's my birthday in September* (lit. *I make years in September*). Go back to the introductory material of this course to remind yourself how to say the months of the year in Portuguese.

4 WORDS OF POSSESSION (*MY, YOUR, OUR*) – AN INTRODUCTORY SUMMARY

The words of possession in Portuguese match the words that are being possessed, not the person, or thing, doing the possessing. Look at the patterns to help you remember them.

	masc. sing.	fem. sing.	masc. pl.	fem. pl.
my	**o meu**	**a minha**	**os meus**	**as minhas**
your	**o seu**	**a sua**	**os seus**	**as suas**
our	**o nosso**	**a nossa**	**os nossos**	**as nossas**

Often, Brazilians leave out the words **o**, **a**, etc.

my father	**(o) meu pai**
your girlfriend	**(a) sua namorada**
our sons / children	**(os) nossos filhos**

Practice 2

1 Find the correct adjective for each expression.

a	É uma casa (*house*)	**1**	gordo (*fat*)
b	Os irmãos são	**2**	bonita
c	O meu pai é	**3**	baratas (*cheap*)
d	As botas (*boots*) são	**4**	velhos

2 Match the Portuguese sentence with its English translation.

a	Ela é mais baixa.	**1**	The fattest cats.
b	Este é o meu irmão mais novo.	**2**	This is my younger brother.
c	Os gatos mais gordos.	**3**	She is shorter.
d	As professoras mais lindas.	**4**	The prettiest teachers.

3 Translate using the verb fazer.

a My birthday's in March.
b His birthday's in December.
c When is your birthday?
d Their birthday (f.) is in August.

4 Change from singular to plural.

a a minha irmã ⟶ _____
b o seu empregado ⟶ _____
c a nossa casa ⟶ _____
d o meu tio (*uncle*) ⟶ _____

Reading and writing

1 Fill in the gaps in the text, choosing the correct word from the box.

> em   tenho   dois   sou
> é   minha   de

Meu nome _____ Ângela dos Santos Macedo. Moro _____ São Paulo, mas sou _____ Taubaté. _____ vinte e cinco anos e _____ solteira. Moro com meu pai, _____ mãe e meus _____ irmãos: Paulo e Flávio. Sou recepcionista no Hotel Transamérica.

2 **According to the text, what are the correct answers to the following questions?**

- **a** How old is Ângela?
- **b** Where was she born?
- **c** Is she married or single?
- **d** Where does she live?

 3 **02.06 Pronunciation practice**

The following words from the conversations all had the letter combination **lh** in them: **filho**, **filha**, **velho**, **olhos**, **trabalha**. This sounds like the *lli* sound in the English word *million*. Listen to these words again now and repeat them, concentrating hard on sounding like the native speaker.

Go further

Here are some further phrases to describe yourself and other people:

eu tenho …	*I have …*
ele / ela tem…	*he / she has …*
cabelos brancos / grisalhos	*white / grey hair*
cabelos longos	*long hair*
cabelos curtos	*short hair*
barba	*beard*
bigode	*moustache*
eu sou …	*I am …*
ele / ela é …	*he / she is …*
careca	*bald*
eu uso …	*I wear / use*
ele / ela usa…	*he / she wears / uses*
óculos	*glasses*
lentes de contato	*lenses*
chapéu	*hat*
bengala	*walking stick, cane*

Could you describe yourself, using the vocabulary given?

Eu tenho cabelos _____, olhos _____. Sou _____.

Uso / Não uso _____.

Listen and understand

 02.07 **Listen to three people describing their relatives and identify them amongst the pictures.**

(a)

(b)

(c)

(d)

(e)

? Test yourself

1 Follow the clues and choose the correct words from the box.

> pais   solteiros   marido   mãe

  a Ela é casada; o _____ chama-se Luís.
  b Eu sou filha dos (of) meus _____.
  c Os amigos não são casados; são _____.
  d A nossa _____ é dona de casa.

2 Lonely hearts – Ana wants to meet someone tall, with green eyes and dark hair. Who should she pick?

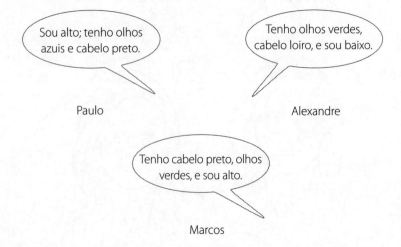

Sou alto; tenho olhos azuis e cabelo preto.

Paulo

Tenho olhos verdes, cabelo loiro, e sou baixo.

Alexandre

Tenho cabelo preto, olhos verdes, e sou alto.

Marcos

3 **02.08** Numbers: listen and circle which numbers you hear.

12 **38** **63** **100** **16** **41** **74** **2** **22** **57** **85** **99**

4 Have a go at saying these out loud in Portuguese.

  a Are you married? (to a woman)
  b How old are you? (sing.)
  c Do you have children?
  d How beautiful! (about a man)
  e Where is he studying?

SELF CHECK

I CAN ...

- ○ . . . talk about how old people are.
- ○ . . . talk about my family.
- ○ . . . express marital status.
- ○ . . . use numbers from 0 to 100.
- ○ . . . describe people.
- ○ . . . discuss where people are studying.

O que você recomenda?

What do you recommend?

In this unit, you will learn how to:
▶ *order drinks and snacks.*
▶ *express likes and dislikes.*
▶ *order a meal in a restaurant.*
▶ *discuss typical dishes and how they are served.*
▶ *ask for suggestions and recommendations.*
▶ *find your way round a Brazilian menu.*

CEFR: (A1) *Can recognize familiar names, words and very basic phrases on simple notices (menus);* **(A2)** *Can say what he / she likes and dislikes; Can order a meal.*

 A cozinha brasileira

Brazilian cuisine is varied and heavily influenced by African, Indian and European origins. An enormous variety of fruits, vegetables and types of flour are used to create different dishes, not to mention the abundance of good quality meat and excellent fish. Greater African influence is found in the north-east – **muitos pratos** (*many dishes*) made with tapioca, **carne de sol** (*Brazilian sundried meat*) and **azeite de dendê** (*palm oil*) such as **acarajé** (*black-eyed pea fritters*) and **vatapá** (*a kind of shrimp curry with a sauce made from onions, peanuts, cashews and coconut milk, and thickened with breadcrumbs*); in the north, many dishes are made with **peixes** (*fish*) found in Amazonian rivers. In the south-east and the south one can try a great diversity of dishes due to the influence of foreign immigrants. A fruit called **pequi**, native to the Centre-West and North-East regions, is used a lot in the state of Goiás and in the north-east, and is eaten in dishes with rice or chicken. Also typical of Goiás is the **empadão goiano**, (*a savoury tart with a filling of chicken pieces*) and / or **linguiça** (*pork sausage*). **Feijoada** (*black bean stew with pieces of pork*) and **churrasco** (*barbecued meat*) are eaten throughout the country.

There are various popular beliefs around the kitchen, such as the **boa mão** (*good hand*) and the **má mão** (*bad hand*). To have a 'good hand' means the cook can prepare excellent food, while someone with a **má mão** cannot get any dish right and is a disaster in the kitchen.

Can you guess what this sentence means? **A feijoada da Joana é excelente! Ela tem uma boa mão!**

Vocabulary builder

03.01 Look at the words and phrases and complete the missing English expressions. Then listen and try to imitate the pronunciation of the speakers.

BEBIDAS	*DRINKS*
uma cerveja	*a beer*
um chope	*a draught beer*
uma água mineral	*a _____ water*
uma garrafa de vinho tinto / branco	*a bottle of red / white _____*
um guaraná	*a guaraná* (type of plant-based soft drink)
uma caipirinha	*a caipirinha* (cocktail made from the sugar cane spirit called cachaça, lime juice, sugar and crushed ice)
um suco de maracujá	*a passion fruit juice*
uma batida	*a cocktail* (usually made from condensed milk, fruit and alcohol)
uma batida de côco	*a coconut cocktail*
um cafezinho	*an espresso*
um café com leite	*a coffee with milk*
um chá com leite	*a tea with _____*

COMIDAS	*FOOD / SNACKS*
um sanduíche de queijo / presunto / ovo	*a cheese / ham / egg _____*
um bauru	*a sandwich traditionally made using French bread, with slices of roast beef, tomatoes, pickles and melted cheese*
um hambúrguer / x-búrguer	*a hamburger / cheeseburger*
uma porção de mandioca frita	*a portion of fried cassava chips*
batatas fritas	*chips, fries*
uma coxinha	*a large deep-fried chicken and potato cake*
uma esfirra	*a Lebanese-style bread cake with minced meat filling*

um bolo de limão	*a lemon cake*
um sorvete de morango	*a strawberry ice cream*
um mousse de chocolate	*a _____ mousse*

 NEW EXPRESSIONS

 03.02 Look at the words and expressions that are used in the following conversation. Note their meanings.

Vamos beber alguma coisa?	*Shall we have something to drink?*
O que você quer?	*What do you want?*
Eu quero …	*I want …*
Não sei	*I don't know*
Não gosto muito de cerveja	*I don't like beer very much*
Talvez um suco	*Perhaps a fruit juice*
Você precisa experimentar os sucos daqui	*You need to try the juices here*
São muito gostosos!	*They're very delicious / tasty!*
O que você sugere então?	*What do you suggest then?*
Que tal …?	*How / What about …?*
E para comer?	*And to eat?*
Posso ver o cardápio?	*Can I see the menu?*
Você não deveria perder	*You shouldn't miss*
Divido com você	*I'll share with you*
Vou pedir um bauru também	*I'm going to order a bauru as well*
o garçom	*the waiter*
Pois não?	*Can I help you?*

Conversation 1

 03.03 Mariana and Jorge pop into a snack bar to order drinks and a snack.

1 What does Jorge want to drink?

Jorge	Mariana, vamos beber alguma coisa? Estou com sede.
Mariana	Tudo bem, Jorge. O que você quer?
Jorge	Eu quero um chope, e você?
Mariana	Não sei; não gosto muito de cerveja. Talvez um suco.
Jorge	Ah, sim, você precisa experimentar os sucos daqui – são muito gostosos!
Mariana	Ah é? O que você sugere então?
Jorge	Que tal um suco de maracujá, banana e limão?

Mariana	Ótimo! E para comer? Eu estou com fome. Posso ver o cardápio, Jorge?
Jorge	Aqui. Você não deveria perder a mandioca frita – é muito boa.
Mariana	Tudo bem, divido com você. Vou pedir um bauru também. E você?
Jorge	Eu quero um x-búrguer. [pause] Aqui vem o garçom.
(The waiter approaches.)	
Garçom	Boa tarde. Pois não?
Jorge	Boa tarde. Um bauru, um x-búrguer e uma porção de mandioca frita.
Garçom	E para beber?
Mariana	Um suco de maracujá, banana e limão, e um chope. Obrigada.

> **LANGUAGE TIP**
>
> The letter **x** in the Portuguese alphabet is pronounced *sheesh*; a **x-búrguer** is supposed to sound like *cheeseburger*!

2 Read the conversation again and, with the help of the new expressions, answer the questions.

a What does Jorge suggest to Mariana that she should drink?

b What does Jorge say is very good?

c What time of day does the conversation take place?

 3 03.04 Now listen to the exchange with the waiter again, and supply Jorge and Mariana's words.

Garçom	Boa tarde. Pois não?
Jorge	Say: *Good afternoon. A bauru, a cheeseburger and a portion of fried cassava.*
Garçom	E para beber?
Mariana	Say: *A passion fruit, banana and lemon juice, and a draught beer. Thanks.*

Saúde! / Tchin tchin!	*Cheers!*
com gelo / sem gelo	*with ice / without ice*
com gás / sem gás	*fizzy / still* (lit. *with / without gas*)

 Language discovery 1

1. **Which Portuguese verb forms mean** *you want / I want / Can I (I can)*?

2. **Jorge describes the fruit juices as muito gostosos and the fried cassava as muito boa; what is the word muito adding to the descriptions?**

3. **If não gosto means** *I don't like*, **what do you think is the expression for** *I like*?

1 THE VERBS *TO WANT / TO HAVE TO / TO BE ABLE TO* – **QUERER / DEVER / PODER**

Look at how these Portuguese verbs are formed in the present tense:

	eu	você	ele / ela	nós	vocês	eles / elas
querer *(to want / wish)*	quero	quer	quer	queremos	querem	querem
dever *(to have to / must)*	devo	deve	deve	devemos	devem	devem
poder *(to be able to / can)*	posso	pode	pode	podemos	podem	podem

Remember that rising intonation at the end of a statement will turn what you are saying into a question:

Podemos fumar aqui.	*We can smoke here.*
Podemos fumar aqui?	*Can we smoke here?*

As well as expressing a need to do something, **dever** is also used to suppose something:

Ela deve estar com sede.	*She must be thirsty.*

It also means *to owe*:

Eles devem 30 reais.	*They owe 30 reals.*

---

você deve *you must*; **você deveria** *you ought to*
você pode *you can*; **você poderia** *you could*
eu quero *I want*; **eu queria** *I would like*
It is not considered impolite to say **quero** when asking for things.

---

2 ADDING EXTRAS TO DESCRIPTIONS: SAYING SOMETHING IS
VERY / A LITTLE / QUITE / REALLY

When you want to add to a description of something, either to emphasize or intensify what the item is like, you can use the following expressions:

muito	*very*	**muito bom**	*very good*
um pouco	*a little / a little bit*	**um pouco caro**	*a bit expensive*

bastante	quite	**bastante mau**	quite bad
realmente	really / indeed	**realmente gostoso**	really tasty

The words for *good* and *bad* in Portuguese change according to the rules of masculine/ feminine and singular / plural as follows:

masc. sing.	fem. sing.	masc. pl.	fem. pl.
bom	boa	bons	boas
mau	má	maus	más

Brazilians also use the word **ruim** a lot to describe something that is *bad* or *awful*:

esta música é ruim	*this music is awful*

3 EXPRESSING LIKES AND DISLIKES

gosto	*I like*
não gosto	*I don't like*
gosto mais de …	*I like … more*
prefiro	*I prefer*
adoro	*I adore / love*
destesto	*I detest*
odeio	*I hate*
não suporto	*I can't stand*

Gostar (*to like*) needs the word **de** after it when the verb is followed by the name of what you like: **gosto de vinho** *I like wine*; **gosto de dançar** *I like to dance*. In answer to someone's question, you simply use the verb form without the **de**:

Você gosta de queijo?	*Do you like cheese?*
Eu gosto, sim. / Sim, gosto.	*Yes I do.*

Practice 1

1 Use a verb from the box to complete each of the sentences.

> quer   devem   posso   deveria

- **a** Eu _____ experimentar?
- **b** O que você _____ beber?
- **c** Você não _____ fumar aqui.
- **d** Elas _____ estar com calor.

2 Supply the correct words to enhance the descriptions.

a O sorvete daqui é _____ (*really*) gostoso.

b A Mônica é _____ (*quite*) bonita.

c Os produtos são _____ (*a little*) caros.

d Meus primos têm um cachorro (*dog*) _____ (*very*) inteligente.

3 Choose the correct form of the words for *good* and *bad*.

a Estes sucos são bons / boas.

b Minha irmã é muito mau / má.

c Meu celular novo (*new*) é boa / bom.

d Os cigarros (*cigarettes*) são maus / más para a saúde (*health*).

 4 03.05 **Listen to three people say what food and drink they like or dislike, and complete the table.**

	Food or drink	Likes or dislikes?
a		
b		
c		

Conversation 2

 NEW EXPRESSIONS

 03.06 **Look at the words and expressions that are used in the following conversation. Note their meanings.**

para começar	*for starters* (lit. *in order to start*)
para mim	*for me*
canja	*chicken broth*
uma saladinha de palmito	*a small salad of heart of palm*
picanha com feijão	*rump steak with black beans*
a especialidade da casa	*the house speciality*
Qual é o acompanhamento?	*What does it come with?* (lit. *What is the accompaniment?*)
porco grelhado	*grilled pork*
beterraba	*beetroot*
cenoura	*carrot*
uma garrafa do vinho da casa	*a bottle of the house wine*
pavê de abacaxi	*creamy biscuit tart with pineapple*
arroz doce	*rice pudding*
Sou alérgico/a (a / ao …)	*I'm allergic (to …)*

03.07 *André and Teresa order a meal in a restaurant.*

Read and listen to the conversation, then answer the questions.

1   What does André order to accompany his main course?

Garçom	Boa noite! Então?
André	Boa noite! Bom, para começar, uma canja e uma saladinha de palmito.
Garçom	Muito bem , e depois?
André	Para mim, a picanha com feijão, e uma salada de tomate. E você, Teresa? O que você quer?
Teresa	Não sei. *(to the waiter)* O que você recomenda?
Garçom	Bom, tem a especialidade da casa – porco grelhado. É muito bom!
Teresa	Qual é o acompanhamento?
Garçom	Vem com arroz, batatas fritas e uma salada de beterraba.
Teresa	Sou alérgica a beterraba. Pode ser cenoura?
Garçom	Sem problema. Agora, para beber?
André	Uma garrafa do vinho da casa.
Garçom	Tinto ou branco?
André	Tinto. E uma garrafa de água mineral sem gás. Obrigado.
(Later, following the main course …)	
Garçom	Vocês querem sobremesa?
Teresa	O que tem?
Garçom	Tem mousse de maracujá, pavê de abacaxi, salada de frutas e arroz doce.
Teresa	Então queria o pavê. André, o que você quer?
André	Eu divido com você – não estou com muita fome.
Garçom	Cafezinho?
André	Dois por favor, e a conta.

2   Read the conversation again and answer the following questions.
   a What comes with the grilled pork?
   b What kind of wine do they order?
   c Which dessert does Teresa want?

Language discovery 2

1 **Look at the expression from the conversation for a bottle of the house wine (lit. a bottle of the wine of the house): uma garrafa do vinho da casa. Why do you think do and da are different?**

2 **What expression does André use to say** *I'll share with you* **?**

3 **Which words in the conversation mean** *grilled / fried* **?**

1 *OF, OF THE* – **DE, DO, DA**

The Portuguese word for *of* or *from* is **de**. When it's followed by any of the words for *the* (which you learned in Unit 2), the words combine, or contract, as follows:

de	+o	+a	+os	+as
	do	**da**	**dos**	**das**

uma salada de rúcola	*a rocket salad*
gosto da sopa	*I like the soup*
uma porção das batatas	*a portion of the potatoes*

2 -IR VERBS, PRESENT TENSE: **DIVIDIR** *TO DIVIDE, SHARE*

Regular **-ir** ending verbs in Portuguese form the present tense as follows:

Remove the **-ir** then add these endings to the stem. Follow the example for the verb **dividir**:

eu divido	**nós dividimos**
você (etc.) divide	**vocês dividem**
ele / ela divide	**eles / elas dividem**

There are fewer regular **-ir** verbs than **-ar** and **-er** ones. Many have irregular spellings in parts of the verb. However, common regular examples include: **abrir** (*to open*), **decidir** (*to decide*) and **partir** (*to depart / to break*).

3 DESCRIBING FOOD: USING MORE ADJECTIVES

Many words used to describe the way food has been cooked, prepared or presented are adjectives and you need to remember to change their endings to match (or agree with) the food item being described.

grelhado (*grilled*), **frito** (*fried*), **assado** (*roasted / baked*), **frio** (*cold*), **recheado** (*filled*), **cozido** (*boiled*) all follow the regular pattern of changing the last letter **-o** to **-a / -os / -as**.

doce (*sweet*), **picante** (*spicy*), **quente** (*hot = not cold*) don't change the final **-e** but do add an **-s** for the plurals (masculine and feminine).

The word for *raw*, **cru**, changes to **crua** in the feminine and adds an **-s** for the plurals.

carne assada (*roast meat*), **ovos recheados** (*stuffed eggs*), **camarões picantes** (*spicy shrimps*), **peixe cru** (*raw fish*).

Practice 2

1 Complete with the correct form: de / do / da / dos / das.
   a Uma garrafa do vinho _____ casa.
   b O professor _____ alunos (*pupils*).
   c Uma sopa _____ cenoura.
   d O preço (*price*) _____ botas.
   e O consultório (*surgery*) _____ médico.

2 Translate.
   a I'll share with you.
   b The bank opens tomorrow (**amanhã**).
   c We do not depart today (**hoje**).
   d Roberta decides to drink water.

3 Match the correct adjective to the items of food.

a	peixe	**1**	assadas
b	molhos	**2**	crua
c	batatas	**3**	frito
d	carne	**4**	picantes

Listen and understand

 03.08 Márcia and Guilherme are at a Praça da Alimentação (*food court***) of a shopping mall in Brasília. They try to decide where to eat. Find out what kind of food each one prefers. The restaurants mentioned (Marietta and Montana Grill) are Brazilian restaurant chains, found mainly in food courts of large shopping centres, but also in some city centres.**

Márcia chooses: _____

Guilherme chooses: _____

Reading and writing

comida mineira	*food from the state of Minas Gerais*
comida baiana	*food from the state of Bahia*
polenta	*cornmeal boiled in water into a porridge (similar to Italian polenta)*
feijão tropeiro	*'Minas Gerais style cattleman's beans' – beans, pieces of bacon, linguiça (pork sausage) and manioc flour*

1 Fill in the gaps in the text, choosing the correct word from the box.

> comida adoramos peixe
> favorito adoro

Júlia and her husband's favourite foods:

Eu _____ comida mineira, mas o meu marido prefere _____ baiana.

Meu prato _____ é polenta com feijão tropeiro e linguiça. Meu marido prefere pratos com _____ e camarão, e molhos picantes que eu não gosto. Nós dois _____ comer numa churrascaria!

2 True or false?

    a Júlia does not like spicy food.

    b Júlia's husband loves food from Bahia.

    c Neither Júlia nor her husband likes barbecued meat.

3 03.09 Pronunciation practice

The following words from the conversations all had the letter combination **ão** in them: **não**, **são**, **então**, **limão**, **porção**. This sounds like a very nasal *ow* as in the English word *cow*. Try to say it as though you have a blocked nose! Listen to these words again now and repeat them, concentrating hard on sounding like the native speaker.

Go further

If you visit Brazil, you must try the delicious fresh fruit juices made **em casa** (*at home*) and in **lanchonetes** (*snack bars*). Two, three or more fresh fruits are mixed in front of your eyes and the combinations are endless. The most common are:

abacaxi com hortelã	*pineapple and mint*
abacaxi com gengibre	*pineapple and ginger*
laranja com acerola	*orange and acerola berry*
açaí com banana	*açaí berry and banana*
açaí com morango e maçã	*açaí berry, strawberry and apple*

Equally delicious are the many ice creams made of different combinations of tropical fruits and nuts. The traditional chocolate, vanilla and strawberry flavours can also be found.

As for commercially-made drinks, Brazil has **guaraná** (a refreshing fizzy drink made with the Amazonian fruit **guaraná**). It competes with Coca-Cola and Pepsi and can be bought in supermarkets and restaurants. The most famous alcoholic drink is the **caipirinha** (pronounced kai-pee-REEN-yuh), a cocktail made of **cachaça** (a sugar-cane based spirit similar to white rum), lime juice, sugar and crushed ice. **Cachaça** is also known by other names, such as **pinga** and **aguardente**. Drink it in small doses!

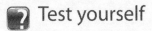 Test yourself

1 Complete the menu with the missing words.

> ## Restaurante Fluminense
> ### Cardápio
>
> **Entradas**
>
> canja
>
> salada de _____ (*carrot*)
>
> sopa de tomate
>
> **Especialidade da casa:**
>
> **Sobremesas**
>
> salada de frutas
>
> pavê
>
> arroz _____ (*sweet*)
>
> **Pratos principais**
>
> picanha com feijão
>
> xinxim de galinha (*spicy chicken stew*)
>
> _____ (*fish*) grelhado
>
> porco _____ (*roasted*)
>
> **Bebidas**
>
> cerveja
>
> vinho da casa – _____ (*white*)
>
> – tinto
>
>

2 03.10 Listen to Silvana ordering a meal and note what she asks for:

Starter:

Main meal with accompaniment:

Dessert:

Drink:

3 Complete your part of the dialogue with a waiter and practise saying it out loud.

Garçom	Bom dia. Pois não?
You	Say: *Good morning. A ham sandwich and a portion of fried cassava, please.*
Garçom	E para beber?
You	Say: *An orange and acerola juice.*

SELF CHECK

I CAN ...

- ... order drinks and snacks.
- ... express likes and dislikes.
- ... order a meal in a restaurant.
- ... discuss typical dishes and how they are served.
- ... ask for suggestions and recommendations.
- ... find my way round a Brazilian menu.

R1 Review 1

1 Complete with the correct forms of either ser, estar or ter.

  a Eu _____ brasileiro.

  b Vocês não _____ filhos?

  c Paulo _____ com sede.

  d Nós _____ engenheiros.

  e Você _____ um cardápio?

  f Onde _____ os meus óculos?

2 Which questions would you ask to get these replies? Look carefully at the verbs used in the responses.

a _____ ?	Eu trabalho na universidade.
b _____ ?	Não, o Fernando não come peixe.
c _____ ?	Partimos na sexta-feira.
d _____ ?	Sim, gosto muito de cerveja!
e _____ ?	Não, eles não vendem queijo.

3 Translate into Portuguese.

  a He is tall.

  b My sisters are not fat.

  c She has green eyes.

  d The soup is cold.

  e The fruit juices are delicious.

  f She is very pretty.

4 3.11 Listen to people introducing members of the family, their ages and birthdays, and complete the missing information.

  a Este é o meu _____. Ele tem _____ anos. Faz anos no dia _____ de _____.

  b Esta é a nossa _____. Ela tem _____ anos. Faz anos no dia _____ de _____.

  c Esta é a minha _____. Ela tem _____ anos. Faz anos no dia _____ de _____.

  d Este é o meu _____. Ele tem _____ anos. Faz anos no dia _____ de _____.

  e Esta é a nossa _____. Ela tem _____ anos. Faz anos no dia _____ de _____.

Who is the youngest? Who is the oldest? Whose birthday is in September?

 5 3.12 **Have a go at saying these words out loud, then listen to them on the audio.**

> vinho   senhor   trabalhar   mão
> limão   Espanha   filha   julho
> então   alimentação

6 You and two friends are dining out. Look at the description of what everyone likes or dislikes, then using the menu, choose an appropriate meal for the group.

You: never have starters; don't like fish; love pork; prefer sweet puddings. Like cocktails.

Samuel: prefers cold starters; allergic to seafood; likes chicken best; doesn't have a sweet tooth. Always drinks beer.

Patrícia: vegetarian but can't stand tomatoes; adores ice cream; doesn't drink alcohol.

Restaurante beija-flor
Cardápio

Entradas
canja
salada de palmito
sopa de tomate

Pratos principais
camarões picantes
galinha assada
porco grelhado

Especialidade da casa:
ovos recheados

Sobremesas
salada de frutas
pavê de abacaxi
sorvete (variado)

Bebidas
cerveja
vinho da casa – branco / tinto
caipirinha
sucos – maracujá / açaí com maçã / laranja

	Entrada	Prato principal	Sobremesa	Bebida
You				
Samuel				
Patrícia				

7 **Answer these questions out loud in Portuguese. You will find sample responses in the Answer key.**

a Como vai?

b Como se chama?

c Onde trabalha?

d Você fala francês?

e Onde você mora?

f Qual é o seu email?

g Qual é o número do seu celular?

h De onde você é?

i Você é casado/a?

j Você tem filhos?

k Quantos anos você tem?

l Quando você faz anos?

8 3.13 **Listen to Maria and Bruno talk about themselves, and complete the missing information.**

	Where from	Nationality	Where live	Profession / work	Marital status	Languages spoken	Phone number
Maria			São Paulo			Portuguese, French, English	
Bruno	Family from Italy				Single, but has girlfriend		

9 **You are ordering a meal at a restaurant. Complete your part of the conversation with the waiter by following the cues.**

Garçom	Boa noite! Então?
You	Say *Good evening! For starters, a carrot salad.*
Garçom	Muito bem, e depois?
You	Say *What do you recommend?*
Garçom	Bom, a especialidade da casa é feijoada. É fantástica!
You	Say *I prefer fish.*
Garçom	Então, que tal o nosso vatapá?

You	Say *OK*.
Garçom	E para beber?
You	Say *A bottle of the house wine*.
Garçom	Tinto ou branco?
You	Say *White. And a bottle of fizzy mineral water, please*.
(Later)	
Garçom	Para sobremesa?
You	Say *A chocolate mousse, please*.
Garçom	Cafezinho?
You	Say *Yes please, and the bill*.

A rotina diária

Daily routine

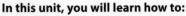

In this unit, you will learn how to:
▶ *describe your habits and routines.*
▶ *talk about daily life.*
▶ *say how often you do things.*
▶ *use days of the week.*
▶ *say the words for different countries.*
▶ *distinguish between the two verbs* to know.

CEFR: (A1) *Can reply in an interview to simple direct questions;* **(A2)** *Can describe habits and routine; Can ask and answer questions about habits and routines.*

 Rotinas típicas

Family life can be very hectic in Brazil, especially in the large cities, where a lot of time is spent in **engarrafamentos** (*traffic jams*) or on two or three buses, between **casa e trabalho** (*home and work*). In general, Brazilians don't eat a lot for **o café da manhã** (*breakfast*). Um **pedaço de pão** (*a piece of bread*) or **uma torrada** (*a piece of toast*) and **uma xícara de café** (*a cup of coffee*) are enough for most people. **O almoço** (*lunch*) is the main meal for most people, who prefer something **mais leve** (*lighter*) in the evening, like a sandwich, rather than a heavy **jantar** (*dinner*). At lunchtime, those who work in cities tend to eat close to their office or eat a meal at the **cantina** (*canteen*) in their workplace, if they work in factories or large companies. Lighter snacks taken during the day are often referred to as a **lanche** (*snack*), not to be confused with the English word *lunch*.

Keeping fit is important and can be a routine obsession. Many like to **ir na academia** (*go to the gym*) **uma vez, duas vezes ou três vezes por semana** (*one, two or three times a week*). At weekends many people **vão à igreja** (*go to church*), eat out and go to the **shopping** (*shopping mall*). Brazilians love to walk around large shopping malls, even if **só para ver as vitrines** (*just for window shopping*), go to the cinema or to eat with family or friends at the **Praça da Alimentação** (*food court*).

Can you understand what Célia is saying here? **De manhã, tomo uma xícara de café e como duas torradas com manteiga antes de ir para o trabalho.**

Vocabulary builder

04.01 **Look at the words and phrases and complete the missing English expressions. Then listen and try to imitate the pronunciation of the speakers.**

FREQUÊNCIA	*FREQUENCY*
todos os dias	*every day* (lit. *all the days*)
o dia todo	*all day long / the whole day*
por (semana / mês / ano)	*per (week / month / year)*
cada (hora / dia)	*each, every (hour / day)*
de manhã	*in the _____*
de tarde	*in the afternoon, in the early evening*
de noite	*at _____*
no fim de semana	*at the weekend*
muitas vezes	*many times, often*
poucas vezes	*rarely, seldom*
sempre	*always*
nunca / quase nunca	*never / hardly ever*
normalmente	*normally, usually*
geralmente	*generally*
raramente	_____

PAÍSES	*COUNTRIES*
o Brasil	*Brazil*
o Canadá	*Canada*
Portugal	*Portugal*
os Estados Unidos	*the USA*
a França	_____
a Espanha	*Spain*
a Inglaterra	*England*
a Alemanha	_____
a China	*China*
a Argentina	*Argentina*

NEW EXPRESSIONS

 04.02 Look at the words and expressions that are used in the following conversation. Note their meanings.

Você está gostando …?	*Are you enjoying …?*
meu horário é bastante diferente	*my timetable is quite different*
na França dou aulas	*in France I give lessons (I teach)*
até de noite	*even at night*
durante o dia	*during the day*
na minha faculdade	*in my faculty*
menos na sexta-feira	*except on a Friday*
passo uma hora lendo os jornais	*I spend an hour reading the papers*
aí saio para conhecer novos lugares	*then I go out to get to know new places*
sei lá	*I've no idea / who knows?*
O que você acha da nossa cidade?	*What do you think of our city?*
Sinceramente, acho grande demais	*Honestly, I find it too big*

Conversation 1

 04.03 Brazilian teacher Eduardo discusses work routines with a visiting French academic, Jean-Paul.

1 Does Jean-Paul teach all day back home in France?

Eduardo	Então, Jean-Paul, você está gostando de São Paulo?
Jean-Paul	Sim, estou gostando, mas meu horário é bastante diferente.
Eduardo	Diferente como?
Jean-Paul	Bem, para começar, na França dou aulas só de manhã; aqui tem aulas também de tarde, e até de noite.
Eduardo	Aqui no Brasil é normal. Muitos estudantes trabalham durante o dia e estudam de noite.
Jean-Paul	Na minha faculdade em Paris trabalho vinte horas por semana. Aqui dou aulas todos os dias menos na sexta-feira.
Eduardo	O que você faz nas sextas, então?
Jean-Paul	Geralmente passo uma hora lendo os jornais; aí saio para conhecer novos lugares; sei lá – talvez tomar uma cerveja.
Eduardo	E o que você acha da nossa cidade, Jean-Paul?
Jean-Paul	Sinceramente, acho grande demais para mim, mas é interessante.

2 **Read the conversation again and, with the help of the new expressions, say whether these statements are true or false.**

a Jean-Paul is not enjoying his visit to São Paulo.

b In Brazil, Jean-Paul teaches every day except Friday.

c He sometimes stops for a beer during his walks around São Paulo.

LANGUAGE TIPS

dar *to give*: **dou**, **dá**, **damos**, **dão**

Countries in Portuguese are either masculine or feminine, and are usually accompanied by the appropriate word for *the*: **o Brasil**, **a Espanha**, etc. Often, though, in the spoken language, these are left out: **Alemanha**, **França**. Some countries, such as Portugal, don't have the word for *the* with them at all.

grande demais	*too big* (lit. *big too much*)
caro demais	*too expensive*
longe demais	*too far*

 ## Language discovery 1

1 **Which word means** *liking / enjoying* **in the following expressions?**

Você está gostando?   Estou gostando

2 **If na França means** *in France*, **which expression in the conversation means** *in Brazil*? **Why do you think there is a difference?**

3 **Which two verbs in the conversation express** *knowing something* **and** *getting to know somewhere*?

1 *-ING* – EXPRESSING AN ACTION GOING ON NOW (THE PRESENT CONTINUOUS FORM)

Use the present tense of the verb **estar**: **estou**, **está**, **estamos**, **estão**, plus make the following changes to the verb of action: remove the **-ar / -er / -ir** ending and replace it with **-ando / -endo / -indo** respectively. This format is used in exactly the same way as the corresponding English, for example:

Estou dormindo.   *I am sleeping.*

Maria está estudando grego.   *Maria is studying Greek.*

2 *IN / ON* WITH COUNTRIES AND DAYS

The word for *in* or *on* (**em**) contracts with the four words for *the* in Portuguese, becoming: **no / na / nos / nas** (*in the / on the*). The expressions are used with countries to say *in*, e.g., **nos Estados Unidos** *in the USA*, and also with days of the week to say *on*, e.g., **na sexta-feira** *on Friday;* **nos sábados** *on Saturdays.* It can also be used to mean *at* – **no fim da semana** *at the weekend.*

Sei lá	*I've no idea, who knows?*
Quem sabe?	*Who knows? / Perhaps*
Não sei	*I don't know*

3 TO KNOW

There are two verbs in Portuguese expressing knowledge: **saber**, used to express *knowing something* or *how to do something*, and **conhecer**, used to express *knowing a person or a place* and *getting to know or be acquainted with people or places*. Look out for a couple of spelling peculiarities in the present tense:

saber: sei / sabe / sabemos / sabem

conhecer: conheço / conhece / conhecemos / conhecem

Você sabe mergulhar?	*Do you know how to dive? (Can you dive?)*
Elas conhecem bem esta cidade.	*They know this city well.*

Practice 1

1 Complete each sentence by correctly forming the parts of estar and the action word to express what people are doing.

- **a** Ela (estar / comer) _____ batatas fritas.
- **b** Vocês (estar / gostar) _____ da visita?
- **c** Eu não (estar / trabalhar) _____ esta semana.
- **d** Nós (estar / partir) _____ agora (*now*).

2 Complete with the correct form: no / na / nos / nas / em.

- **a** Você mora _____ Argentina.
- **b** _____ quintas Miguel estuda marketing.
- **c** Tem um bom filme no cinema _____ sábado.
- **d** _____ Portugal eles comem muito peixe.
- **e** As professoras não trabalham _____ domingos.

3 Match the Portuguese and English.

a	Ela conhece meu primo.	**1**	Does he know how to cook?
b	Ele sabe cozinhar?	**2**	Do you know this place?
c	Não sabemos a resposta.	**3**	She knows my cousin.
d	Você conhece este lugar?	**4**	We don't know the answer.

Conversation 2

NEW EXPRESSIONS

 04.04 **Look at the words and expressions that are used in the following conversation. Note their meanings.**

estamos fazendo uma pesquisa	*we're doing a survey*
Sobre o quê exatamente?	*About what exactly?*
com certeza	*OK, of course*
eu me levanto cedo	*I get up early*
enquanto escuto o rádio	*while I listen to the radio*
a caminho para o trabalho	*on the way to work*
certo	*right / OK*
eu vou muitas vezes à academia	*I often go to the gym*
levanto peso e vou nadar	*I do weightlifting and I go to swim*
me divirto muito	*I have a good time, I enjoy myself*
jantar fora	*to eat out*

04.05 *Gabriela and Sérgio are stopped in the street by someone conducting a survey on habits and routines.*

Read and listen to the conversation, then answer the questions.

1 Do the friends always have breakfast at home?

Entrevistador	Oi gente! Hoje estamos fazendo uma pesquisa – posso fazer algumas perguntas?
Gabriela	Sobre o quê exatamente?
Entrevistador	Sobre sua rotina diária, tá?
Sérgio	Tudo bem, com certeza.
Entrevistador	Legal! Então, vocês sempre tomam café da manhã?
Gabriela	Eu sim. Eu me levanto cedo todos os dias e tomo meu café enquanto escuto o rádio.
Sérgio	Eu não. Raramente como em casa. Eu bebo um cafezinho a caminho para o trabalho.
Entrevistador	E quantas horas vocês trabalham por dia?
Gabriela	Eu trabalho sete horas por dia.
Sérgio	E eu, nove, mas só de segunda a quinta-feira.
Entrevistador	Certo. Quantas vezes por semana vocês fazem exercício?
Sérgio	Eu vou muitas vezes à academia: levanto peso e vou nadar; me divirto muito, sabe? E você, Gabriela?
Gabriela	Ah, eu quase nunca faço exercício. Só na quarta-feira à noite quando gosto de correr um pouco.
Entrevistador	Finalmente, vocês gostam de jantar fora?
Sérgio	Gostamos muito, mas normalmente é só no fim da semana.
Entrevistador	Obrigado. Valeu!

2 Read the conversation again and answer the questions.

  a How many hours a day does Gabriela work?

  b Where does Sérgio do his exercise?

  c What day of the week does Gabriela like to go running?

  d How often do the friends like eating out?

Language discovery 2

1 **What do you think the 'me' means in this expression: Eu me levanto cedo?**

2 **In the conversation, find the Portuguese expression for** *I enjoy myself a lot.*

3 **What is the abbreviated expression for** *Monday* **used in the conversation?**

1 REFLEXIVE VERBS: *I GET (MYSELF) UP, I GET (MYSELF) WASHED*, **ETC.**

When someone carries out the action of a verb on themselves, the Portuguese verb comes with an additional 'reflexive' pronoun, designating the 'self' bit of the verb. These are: **me / se / nos / se**. Observe the difference here:

I wash the car **eu lavo o carro**

I wash myself (i.e., *I get washed*) **eu me lavo**

Look at the whole of the verb *to get (oneself) up* – **levantar-se**:

eu me levanto	*I get up*	**nós nos levantamos**	*we get up*
você se levanta	*you get up* (sing.)	**vocês se levantam**	*you get up* (pl.)
ele / ela se levanta	*he / she / it gets up*	**eles / elas se levantam**	*they get up*

You should be aware that reflexive verbs in Portuguese are not always reflexive in English. You will be able to recognize when a Portuguese verb is reflexive as, if you look it up in a dictionary, you will see that it always has **-se** after the infinitive (the verb with its full **-ar / -er / -ir** ending). Remember not to start a sentence directly with a reflexive pronoun – you need the word for *I, you*, etc. (the subject pronoun) first!

2 REFLEXIVE -IR VERBS WITH IRREGULAR SPELLINGS

Many **-ir** verbs often have irregular spellings in some parts of the verb, and reflexives are no different. Look at some of the common ones here, which all have a change to spelling only in the first person (*I*):

vestir-se *to get dressed*

eu me visto	**nós nos vestimos**
você se veste	**vocês se vestem**
ele / ela se veste	**eles / elas se vestem**

sentir-se *to feel*

eu me sinto

você se sente, etc.

divertir-se *to enjoy oneself*

eu me divirto

você se diverte, etc.

servir-se *to serve / help oneself*

eu me sirvo

você se serve, etc.

3 DAYS – EXPRESSIONS AND ABBREVIATIONS

The five working days of the week can be abbreviated to **segunda**, **terça**, etc. In the written language, the expressions can be shortened even further to **2ª**, **3ª**, **4ª**, etc. and **sáb.**, **dom.**

na quarta(-feira) faço exercício	*on Wednesday I do exercise*
nas sextas gosto de nadar	*on Fridays I like to swim*
da segunda a quinta-feira	*from Monday to Thursday*
cada terça(-feira)	*each Tuesday*
todos os domingos	*every Sunday*

Practice 2

1 Complete with the correct reflexive pronoun: me / se / nos / se.

   a Você _____ diverte na piscina (*in the pool*)?

   b Eu _____ lavo todos os dias.

   c Não _____ levantamos cedo nos domingos.

   d Eles _____ sentem contentes (*happy*).

2 Respond to the questions using the / form of the verbs.

   a Você se sente triste (*sad*)? Não, não _____ triste.

   b Você sempre se diverte na praia? Sim, eu sempre _____.

   c Geralmente você se serve no restaurante? Não, nunca _____.

   d Você se veste de tarde? Não, eu _____ de manhã.

3 04.06 **Listen to Laura describing three of the activities she does during the week, and complete the diary using the expressions in the box.**

> correr na praia   trabalhar
> visitar amigos   jantar fora
> fazer compras (*do the shopping*)

Activity	2ª	3ª	4ª	5ª	6ª	sáb.	dom.
a							
	estudar						
b							
c							
	ver televisão	cozinhar					

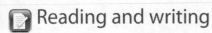

Reading and writing

1 O que ele / ela está fazendo? What is he / she doing?

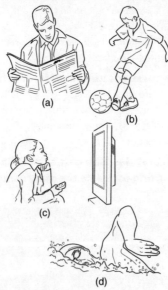

2 Here is a postcard that Samuel wrote to his family back in Brazil. Put each verb into the correct form in Portuguese (equivalent to the *-ing* form in English):

> Oi galera!
>
> Estou _____ (viajar) muito aqui na Europa. Estou _____ (gostar) de tudo! No momento estou _____ (passar) uma semana na Escócia. Estou _____ (comprar) umas lembranças muito bonitas para levar para o Brasil. Tchau!
>
> Um abração,
> Samuel

Oi galera!	*Hi guys! / Hi folks! / Hi everyone!*
lembranças	*souvenirs*
um abraço grande	*lots of love* (lit. *a big hug*)
a Escócia	*Scotland*

3 Fill in each gap with the correct verb from the box.

> estamos gastando (*spending*)
> está comendo   estão vendo
> estou passando   estamos visitando

a Eu _____ três dias em Foz do Iguaçu.
b Nós _____ muitas atrações (*attractions*).
c O Pedro e eu _____ muito dinheiro!
d O Ricardo _____ muito churrasco!
e Vocês _____ as fotos no Facebook?

4   04.07 Pronunciation practice

The following words from the conversations (and many others) all have the letter combination **te**: **bastante**, **diferente**, **noite**, **estudante**, **durante**, **geralmente**. The most common Brazilian pronunciation of this is **tche**, like the *ch* in the English word *church*. You'll hear this particularly in Rio. In parts of southern Brazil and the north-east, the sound is a softer **tuh** sound. Listen to these words again now and repeat them, concentrating hard on sounding like the native speaker.

Listen and understand

04.08 Listen to Ana, a housewife, and answer the questions.

a What does Ana do every day?
b When does she go to the market?
c When does her son have English lessons?
d When does her daughter have ballet lessons?
e Where do the children have lunch every day?

Go further

Can you understand the following text? Try to get the gist of what it is about, or if you feel confident, have a go at translating it into English.

> Eduardo Guedes é um chefe de cozinha famoso no Brasil. Ele é de São Paulo. Ele apresenta um programa de culinária num canal de televisão, de segunda a sexta-feira. Às vezes ele sai do estúdio e viaja para várias partes do Brasil, preparando pratos deliciosos de estados e regiões diferentes. Podemos ver as receitas e os vídeos na internet.

cozinha	*kitchen*
canal de televisão	*TV channel*
receita(s)	*recipe(s)*

Test yourself

1 Unscramble the names of the countries.
   a RGPUOALT
   b PHSANEA
   c ICAHN
   d NÁAADC
   e AANRÇF

2 04.09 Listen and work out which activity each person is describing and indicate how often they do it.

  a Rosana:
  trabalhar / dar aulas de inglês
  35 horas por semana / 25 horas por mês
  b Antônio:
  ver novelas / ir na academia
  muitas vezes / poucas vezes
  c Susana:
  comer o almoço / preparar o café da manhã
  sempre / geralmente não
  d Miguel:
  ir à igreja / ir ao cinema
  todos os domingos / de tarde

3 Have a go at saying these out loud in Portuguese.

  a I work 30 hours a week.
  b On Fridays I eat out.
  c I get up early.
  d I always do exercise on Saturdays.

SELF CHECK

I CAN ...
○ . . . describe my habits and routines.
○ . . . talk about daily life.
○ . . . say how often I do things.
○ . . . use days of the week.
○ . . . say the words for different countries.
○ . . . distinguish between the two verbs *to know*.

5 Tem ônibus para ...?

Is there a bus to ...?

In this unit, you will learn how to:
▶ *ask for, and check, travel information.*
▶ *buy tickets and specify seating.*
▶ *understand numbers from 101 to 1,000.*
▶ *check prices.*
▶ *ask and tell the time.*

CEFR: (A1) *Can handle numbers, cost and time;* **(A2)** *Can get simple information about travel, use public transport and buy tickets; can find specific, predictable information in simple everyday material such as timetables.*

Transportes no Brasil

Trens (*trains*) in Brazil are mostly **para carga** (*for cargo*), carrying minerals and grain from their areas of production to **os portos** (*the ports*). There are a few short lines dedicated to tourism only. Most transport is **por estrada** (*by road*) and some interstate coach journeys can last for more than 30 hours. An **ônibus convencional** (*standard bus / coach*) doesn't always have air conditioning, but does have a toilet, an **ônibus executivo** has reclining seats with more leg room, plus air conditioning, and an **ônibus leito** has air conditioning and seats that recline so you can sleep more comfortably. On long journeys, the buses stop every few hours, and passengers need to pay attention when the **motorista** (*driver*) announces stopping times, such as **'tempo da parada: 20 minutos'** (*stopping for 20 minutes*).

Travelling **de avião** (*by plane*) has become accessible to many Brazilians so more people can afford to fly. In the Amazon region, **barcos e barcas** (*boats and ferries*) cross the many rivers and in some areas these are the only means of transport. In the big cities you can travel **de metrô** (*by underground*). Driving can be a nightmare for foreigners as road maintenance and signalling are not always good, except in **estradas com pedágio** (*toll roads*), which are always in good condition.

 What is the driver telling you? **Tempo da parada: vinte e cinco minutos.**

Vocabulary builder

 05.01 Look at the words and phrases and complete the missing English expressions. Then listen and try to imitate the pronunciation of the speakers.

INFORMAÇÕES DE VIAGEM	*TRAVEL INFORMATION*
uma passagem de ida	*a single ticket*
2 / 3 / 4 passagens	*2 / 3 / 4 tickets*
uma passagem de ida e volta	*a return _____*
um bilhete de metrô	*an underground ticket*
a carteira de estudante	*_____ card*
a carteira de identidade	*identity card (to prove one is older than 65)*
um horário	*a timetable*
a parada	*bus / coach stop*
a plataforma	*platform*
a estação	*station*
a rodoviária	*bus / coach station, terminus*
a linha	*line (for trains or on the underground)*
o próximo …	*the next …*
o último …	*the _____ …*
atrasado	*late*

OS NÚMEROS DE 101 A 1000	*NUMBERS FROM 101 TO 1,000*
cento e um / uma	*101*
duzentos	*200*
trezentos	*300*
quatrocentos	*400*
quinhentos	*500*
seiscentos	*600*
setecentos	*700*
oitocentos	*800*
novecentos	*900*
mil	*1,000*

 NEW EXPRESSIONS

 05.02 Look at the words and expressions that are used in the following conversation. Note their meanings.

Quanto tempo demora a viagem?	*How long does the journey take?*
mais ou menos	*more or less*
A que horas parte?	*At what time does it depart / leave?*

a que horas chega?	*at what time does it arrive?*
Oito e meia da noite	*half-past eight in the evening / at night*
É direto?	*Is it direct?*
você não tem que mudar	*you don't have to change*
Convencional ou executivo?	*Standard or executive (class)?*
um lugar na janela	*a seat by the window*
se possível	*if possible*
Quanto é?	*How much is it?*
O ônibus sai	*The bus leaves*

Conversation 1

 05.03 *Camila is at the bus terminus in Curitiba, enquiring about long-distance buses to Foz do Iguaçu so she can visit the famous waterfalls.*

1 How long does the journey take?

Camila	Boa tarde! Tem ônibus para Foz do Iguaçu?
Empregado	Tem, sim, todos os dias menos no domingo.
(ticket clerk)	
Camila	Ótimo! Quanto tempo demora a viagem?
Empregado	Demora mais ou menos nove horas.
Camila	A que horas parte?
Empregado	Parte às onze e quarenta e cinco.
Camila	E a que horas chega em Foz?
Empregado	Chega às vinte e trinta.
Camila	Tá. Oito e meia da noite. Tudo bem. É direto?
Empregado	É, sim – você não tem que mudar.
Camila	Muito bem, então, uma passagem de ida para amanhã e a de volta para sábado, por favor.
Empregado	Convencional ou executivo?
Camila	Convencional, mas um lugar na janela, se possível. Quanto é com carteira de estudante?
Empregado	São duzentos e cinquenta reais.
Camila	Aqui está!
Empregado	Obrigado. O ônibus sai da plataforma número dezoito.

2 Read the conversation again and, with the help of the new expressions, answer the questions.

  a At what time does the bus arrive in Foz?
  b When does Camila wish to return?
  c What type of discount travel card does Camila have?

3 Now listen to the conversation again, repeating after each line, and concentrating on your pronunciation.

> **LANGUAGE TIPS**
>
> | | |
> |---|---|
> | **Quanto é?** | *How much is it?* |
> | **Quanto custa?** | *How much does it cost?* |
> | **Qual é o preço?** | *What is the price?* |
>
> **Tem ônibus?** is the same as **Há ônibus?** – **há** means *there is / there are*. Many Brazilians, however, use **tem** instead of **há**.
>
> To express means of travel (*by / on*), use **de** before **carro** (**automóvel**) (*car*), **bicicleta** (*bicycle*), **ônibus**, **trem**, **avião**, **metrô**, etc., but **a** before **cavalo** (*horse*) or **pé** (*foot*).

 Language discovery 1

1 If A que horas parte? means *At what time does it leave?*, **which expression in A que horas chega? means** *At what time*?

2 Which two different expressions both mean *eight o'clock at night*?

3 The price of the ticket was duzentos e cinquenta reais (R$250); can you work out how to say *275*?

1 A QUE HORAS …? *AT WHAT TIME …?*

Use **A que horas …?** (lit. *At what hours …?*) whenever you are asking at what time something happens. Notice the word order: **a que horas parte / sai o ônibus para Recife?** (*At what time leaves the bus for Recife? = At what time does the bus for Recife leave?*). The English word *does* is not translated. You can make use of the following verbs, amongst others: **partir** *to depart*; **chegar** *to arrive*; **começar** *to begin*; **terminar / acabar** *to end / finish*; **abrir** *to open*; **fechar** *to close*. **A que horas abre o banco? A que horas termina o filme?**

2 EXPRESSING *AT* **WITH TIME**

Portuguese uses **à** (*at*) with one o'clock and midnight (**meia-noite**), **às** with all hours above one (hours are feminine) and **ao** with midday (**meio-dia**). Minutes past the hour are added on with the word for *and*, **e**, and time to the hour is expressed by **para** *to the hour*.

à uma e dez	*at ten past one*
às duas e quinze	*at 2:15*
à meia-noite e vinte	*at twenty past midnight*
ao meio-dia e meia	*at half past midday*
às cinco para as oito	*at five to eight*

24-hour clock:

dez e quarenta e cinco	**10:45**
vinte e uma e trinta	**21:30**

3 FORMING NUMBERS BETWEEN 100 AND 1,000

Before you start, refresh your memory on the previous set of numbers by going back over them a few times first. Remember that a round *100* = **cem**, but as soon as you creep over the 100 mark, the word becomes **cento** (and you never say **um cento**). The formation sequence uses **e** (*and*) between hundreds, tens and, where necessary, single units:

105	**cento e cinco**
168	**cento e sessenta e oito**
456	**quatrocentos e cinquenta e seis**

Numbers in the hundreds can have a feminine version, if you are counting feminine items:

793 houses	**setecentas e noventa e três casas**

 Practice 1

1 **Complete each sentence by choosing a verb from the first list and a word from the second list.**

parte	concerto
começa	ônibus
abre	banco
chega	avião

a A que horas _____ o _____ de jazz?
b A que horas _____ o _____ leito em Brasília?
c A que horas _____ o _____ para Washington?
d A que horas _____ o _____ do Brasil?

2 Convert the times from the 24-hour clock to the 12-hour clock. Follow the example:

Às 08:25 → Às oito e vinte e cinco (da manhã)

a Às 07:50 —➤ _____
b Às 14:30 —➤ _____
c Às 18:05 —➤ _____
d Às 21:45 —➤ _____
e Às 24:00 —➤ _____

3 Choose the correct version of each number.

a **126** cento e vinte e seis / cento e trinta e seis
b **491** quatrocentos e noventa e um / quinhentos e noventa e um
c **832** oitocentos e três e dois / oitocentos e trinta e dois
d **775** seiscentos e sessenta e cinco / setecentos e setenta e cinco
e **390** trezentos e noventa / trezentos e oitenta

 4 05.04 **Listen to the numbers and order them in sequence as you hear them.**

681   232   242   599   970

Conversation 2

 NEW EXPRESSIONS

 05.05 **Look at the words and expressions that are used in the following conversation. Note their meanings.**

subir outra vez	*to go up again*
e depois descer	*and then to go down*
Com licença	*Excuse me*
Parece que …	*It seems / appears that …*
Que alívio!	*What a relief! / Thank goodness!*
que horas são?	*What time is it?*
Acho que fecha	*I think that it closes*
Chega lá rapidinho	*It gets (lit. arrives) there really quickly*
Obrigado pela ajuda	*Thanks for the help*

05.06 *Rafael is visiting Rio from Recife and wants to visit the Maracanã stadium* (**estádio**); *he needs to catch the metro to Maracanã station, so he checks with other passengers on the platform.*

1 What platform should Rafael be on?

Rafael	Desculpe senhora – sabe se esta é a plataforma certa para o Maracanã?
Senhora	Não é esta, não! Você precisa subir outra vez, e depois descer para a plataforma número cinco.
(Five minutes later, on platform five)	
Rafael	Com licença, você sabe se o trem para o Maracanã está atrasado?
Senhor	Não sei, não, mas tem um horário aqui. Parece que tem trem a cada quinze minutos.
Rafael	Que alívio! Você sabe que horas são agora?
Senhora	São vinte para as duas. Você está visitando o estádio?
Rafael	Estou. E acho que fecha às quatro e quinze.
Senhora	Olhe, aqui vem o trem. Chega lá rapidinho.
Rafael	Obrigado pela ajuda!

2 Read the conversation again and answer the statements with True or False.

a The man on platform five shows Rafael a timetable.

b There are metro trains every quarter of an hour.

c It's now twenty past two.

d The stadium closes at 16:15.

e The woman warns it takes a long time to get there.

---

a cada XX minutos / horas = de XX em XX minutos / horas *every XX minutes / hours*

 # Language discovery 2

1 Which word is used in the text to express *for* **or** *to* **in the following:** *for Maracanã / to platform five / for the help*?

2 When asking and telling the time (*what time is it? / it's …*)**, which of the two Portuguese verbs** *to be* **are used?**

3 Which verb in the text means *comes* **(you've met it before!)?**

1 EXPRESSING *TO* AND *FOR*

Use **para** in expressions denoting direction *to, towards,* or *for*: **o ônibus para Fortaleza** *the bus to / for Fortaleza*; **às vinte para as cinco** *at twenty to five*; **para visitar** *(in order) to visit*; **para o aeroporto por favor** *to the airport, please* (said to a taxi driver); **para mim** *for me*.

Use **por** for expressions using *for, by / along / through, by means of*. **Por** also combines with the words for *the*: **por + o / a / os / as = pelo / pela / pelos / pelas: pelas ruas** *through the streets*; **por avião** *by air* (*by plane* = **de avião**).

obrigado/a pelo convite / presente	*thanks for the invitation / present*
parabéns pelo aniversário / pela promoção	*congratulations on your birthday / your promotion*

2 QUE HORAS SÃO? *WHAT TIME IS IT?*

Use the Portuguese verb **ser** with time:

são X horas / é uma hora / é meio-dia, meia-noite

são duas e quinze / são oito e vinte e cinco / são dez para as seis / são doze horas

é uma e meia / é meio-dia

For clarification, add expressions such as **da manhã** *in the morning*; **da tarde** *in the afternoon / evening*; **da noite** *at night*. **São dez horas da noite. São quinze para as quatro da manhã.**

3 THE VERBS *TO COME* AND *TO GO* – VIR AND IR

	eu	você	ele/ela	nós	vocês	eles / elas
vir	**venho**	**vem**	**vem**	**vimos**	**vêm**	**vêm**
ir	**vou**	**vai**	**vai**	**vamos**	**vão**	**vão**

> **LANGUAGE TIP**
>
> Tickets, tickets! All Brazilians understand the word **bilhete**, but tend to use this mainly for underground tickets; use **passagem** for other travel tickets; for entry tickets to theatres and venues, use **ingresso**.

Practice 2

1 Complete with the appropriate form of por or para.

   a _____ mim, um guaraná.

   b Vamos passar _____ Belo Horizonte.

   c O ônibus _____ Caxambu parte às 10:30.

   d Sabrina gosta de correr _____ parque (*park*).

   e São dez _____ as cinco.

2 Give the following times using the 24-hour clock.

   a É uma hora da tarde.

   b São sete horas e cinquenta e cinco da manhã.

   c São duas e meia da tarde.

   d São dez horas da noite.

3 Choose the correct form of the verbs vir / ir.

   a Eu vou / vai visitar minha prima.

   b Nós vão / vamos chegar às oito horas.

   c Roberta vem / vêm agora.

   d Os estudantes vêm / vem para a festa (*party*).

   e Vocês vou / vão para a praia?

Reading and writing

1 Como ele / ela vai? Fill in the gaps with the correct form of the verb ir and the means of transport.

   a O João _____ para o trabalho de _____

   b Eu _____ para o parque de _____

   c Nós _____ para Salvador de _____

(a)

(b)

(c)

2 Look at the following timetable and complete the activity.

Horário dos ônibus do Rio de Janeiro para Belo Horizonte				
Hora saída	Chegada prevista	Preço	Tipo	Empresa
8:45	16:30	R$130	leito	Útil
11:00	17:30	R$85	convencional	Cometa
14:45	21:45	R$130	leito	Útil
16:00	22:40	R$85	convencional	Cometa

previsto/a	*scheduled*
tipo	*type, kind (of bus)*
empresa	*company*

Now complete the dialogue between you and the employee at the desk at the rodoviária (*bus station*) **in Rio:**

You Ask *Is there a bus to Belo Horizonte in the morning?*

Employee Sim, há um ônibus leito que sai às oito e quarenta e cinco, e um ônibus convencional que sai às onze horas.

You Ask *How much is the ônibus leito?*

Employee São cento e trinta reais, só ida.

You Say *I want two tickets for Friday morning.*

Employee Aqui estão. São duzentos e sessenta reais. Boa viagem!

05.07 **Now practise saying your part out loud. When you feel ready, listen to the audio and try it out.**

3 **Que horas são? Work out the correct times.**

(a)

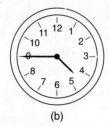
(b)

(c)

4 05.08 **Pronunciation practice**

The following words from the conversations had the letter combination **gem** in them: **viagem**, **passagem**. This sounds like **zhaym**: it's a soft **g (zh)** and a final **m** that's nasal in sound. Listen to these words again now, along with some additional examples, and repeat them, concentrating hard on sounding like the native speaker.

Listen and understand

05.09 **Listen to Cristina describing what she has to do today and answer the questions.**

   a What time does Cristina have a dental appointment?

   b What time does she have a meeting (**reunião**) at the office (**escritório**)?

   c What time does she have to return home to get her suitcase (**pegar a mala**)?

   d What time is her flight (**vôo**) to Brasília?

Go further

Look at the following text about the different fusos horários
(*time zones*) **in Brazil, getting the gist from it first. Then answer the
questions.**

horário de verão	*summer time*
ilha	*island*
a menos	*less*
a menos que em (Brasília)	*behind (Brasília)*
até	*until*

O Brasil tem três fusos horários. Quando é meio dia em Brasília
(horário oficial), também é meio dia em todos os estados das
regiões Nordeste, Sudeste e Sul, e nos estados de Goiás,
Tocantins, Pará e Amapá. Na ilha de Fernando de Noronha, no
Oceano Atlântico, é uma hora da tarde; em todos os estados da
região norte, exceto Pará e Amapá, e nos estados de Mato Grosso
e Mato Grosso do Sul, que ficam a oeste de Brasília, são 11 horas
da manhã – uma hora a menos que em Brasília.

Todos os anos o horário de verão começa no primeiro domingo de
outubro e vai até o último domingo de fevereiro.

1 Complete the statements.

  a Brazil has _____ time zones.

  b When it is midday in Goiás, it's _____ on the island of Fernando
de Noronha.

  c Mato Grosso is one hour _____ Brasília.

  d Official summer time in Brazil ends on the _____ of February.

2 Go back to the map of Brazil at the beginning of the course and try to answer the questions.

  a O jogo de futebol começa às quatro horas da tarde no estádio do
Maracanã, no Rio de Janeiro. A que horas as pessoas em Manaus
devem ligar (switch on) a televisão para ver este jogo?

    1 às 5 horas

    2 às 4 horas

    3 às 3 horas

b Dona Elza mora em São Paulo. Ela telefona para o filho, João, que está de férias em Fernando de Noronha. São nove horas da noite em São Paulo. Que horas são em Fernando de Noronha?

1 **8 horas**

2 **9 horas**

3 **10 horas**

 Test yourself

1 Choose the odd one out.

a passagem	bilhete	horário
b ônibus	plataforma	trem
c para	por	pelos
d vou	vamos	venho

2 Match the questions and answers.

a Quanto é?	**1**	Parte às 18:50.
b A que horas parte?	**2**	São dez e quinze.
c Quanto tempo demora a viagem?	**3**	São dez reais.
d Que horas são?	**4**	Demora seis horas.

3 05.10 Listen to some travel information and complete the missing details.

	destino	parte	plataforma
a	Corumbá	_____	6
b	_____	15:25	8
c	Ouro Prêto	07:50	_____

SELF CHECK

I CAN ...

- ... ask for, and check, travel information.
- ... buy tickets and specify seating.
- ... understand numbers from 101 to 1,000.
- ... check prices.
- ... ask and tell the time.

6 Onde é o Hotel Recife Plaza?

Where is the Recife Plaza Hotel?

In this unit, you will learn how to:
▶ *ask where shops and places are.*
▶ *understand basic directions and instructions.*
▶ *request further assistance.*
▶ *find your way around a Brazilian shopping centre.*
▶ *understand expressions of location.*

CEFR: (A1) *Can understand instructions addressed carefully and slowly, and follow short, simple directions (written or spoken);* **(A2)** *Can ask very simply for repetition when he / she does not understand; Can ask for and give directions referring to a map or a plan.*

No centro da cidade

The city centres of Rio, São Paulo and Belo Horizonte tend to be **o centro financeiro e comercial** (*the financial and commercial centre*), but also where old **edifícios** (*buildings*) with old-style, colonial architecture can be found, alongside modern skyscrapers. City dwellers tend to live in **apartamentos**, sometimes with 10, 15 or even 20 **andares** (*floors*). Many **prédios de apartamentos** (*apartment buildings*) have a **garagem no subsolo** (*underground garage*). Shady places with benches can be found in many parts of the cities and towns, in **parques**, **jardins e praças** (*parks, gardens and squares*), where it is possible to sit down, rest a while and find shade from the strong sun. It is not easy to find a parking space **no centro da cidade** (*in the city centre*), **nos hospitais** (*in hospitals*) and in public service buildings, so sometimes it is less stressful to go by bus and get off at a **ponto de ônibus** (*bus stop*) near the centre; some people choose to go **de táxi**.

Can you understand Paulo's address?
Avenida Cabo Frio, 250 ap. 602
Jardim Alvorada
860620-630 Londrina, PR
Check the Answer Key to see if you're right.

Vocabulary builder

 06.01 Look at the words and phrases and complete the missing English expressions. Then listen and try to imitate the pronunciation of the speakers.

NO CENTRO DA CIDADE	*IN THE CITY CENTRE*
o correio	*post office*
o supermercado	*supermarket*
o mercado	_____
o hospital	*hospital*
o museu	*museum*
o centro cultural	*cultural centre*
o centro de convenções	*conference* _____
a farmácia	*chemist's*
a livraria	*bookshop*
a catedral	*cathedral*
a Central de Informação Turística (CIT)	*tourist information centre*
a rua	*street / road*
o jardim	*garden / small park*
o quarteirão	*block*
a esquina	*corner*
o sinal de trânsito	_____ *lights*

DIREÇÕES	*DIRECTIONS*
à esquerda	*(to / on the) left*
à direita	*(to / on the) right*
em frente	*ahead / in* _____
perto	*near / nearby*
longe	_____
lá /ali	*there /over there*

tomar	to take
pegar	to take
virar	to turn
seguir	to follow / to carry on
cruzar	to cross
atravessar	to cross

 NEW EXPRESSIONS

 06.02 **Look at the words and expressions that are used in the following conversation. Note their meanings.**

É bastante complicado	It's quite complicated
Meu Deus!	Goodness me!
Pode repetir um pouco mais devagar?	Can you repeat that a little more slowly?
É longe, né?	It's a long way, isn't it?
Verdade!	It certainly is! (lit. True!)
Seria melhor …	It would be better …
perguntar de novo	to ask again
Poderia me indicar neste mapa?	Could you show me on this map?
A senhora está vendo aquele sinal de trânsito?	Can you see (lit. Are you seeing) that set of traffic lights?

Conversation 1

06.03 *Hilary Gregson, an Australian visitor to Recife, needs help to locate her hotel, so she asks a man in the city centre.*

1 Which square does Hilary have to cross?

Hilary	Desculpe! O senhor sabe onde é o Hotel Recife Plaza?
Senhor	O Hotel Recife Plaza? Bem, é bastante complicado. A senhora tem que virar aqui, à esquerda, passar pela Praça da República, cruzar a Avenida Boa Vista, e o hotel é na esquina.
Hilary	Meu Deus! Pode repetir um pouco mais devagar, por favor?
Senhor	Claro. (more slowly) A senhora vira aqui, à esquerda, passa pela Praça da República, cruza a Avenida Boa Vista, e o hotel é na esquina.
Hilary	Uf! É longe, né?
Senhor	Verdade! Seria melhor a senhora ir até a praça e perguntar de novo.

(Fifteen minutes later, in the Praça da República …)

Hilary	Por favor! Poderia me indicar neste mapa onde é o Hotel Recife Plaza?
Senhora	Sim, claro. A senhora está vendo aquele sinal de trânsito ali?
Hilary	Estou, sim.
Senhora	Então, precisa seguir em frente, mais ou menos cinquenta metros, e o hotel é no próximo quarteirão.
Hilary	Muito obrigada!

2 Read the conversation again, and with the help of the new expressions, answer the questions.

   a What is the first instruction given to Hilary?

   b What does the man suggest would be better for Hilary to do?

   c What does the woman ask Hilary?

3 6.04 Now listen to the exchange with the woman again and this time supply Hilary's words. You will hear the correct version on the audio.

Hilary	*Excuse me! Could you show me on this map where the Hotel Recife Plaza is?*
Senhora	Sim, claro. A senhora está vendo aquele sinal de trânsito ali?
Hilary	*I am, yes.*
Senhora	Então, precisa seguir em frente, mais ou menos cinquenta metros, e o hotel é no próximo quarteirão.
Hilary	*Thanks very much!*

LANGUAGE TIPS

Onde é …? *Where is …?* and **Onde são …?** *Where are …?* are used for permanent fixtures, such as buildings; for anything that can move position, such as people or objects, use **Onde está …?** and **Onde estão …?**.

primeiro/a	*first*
segundo/a	*second*
terceiro/a	*third*
quarto/a	*fourth*
quinto/a	*fifth*

Don't forget to use the correct masculine or feminine version: **a terceira rua** *the third street*; **o quinto quarteirão** *the fifth block*.

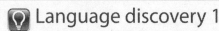

1 **Find the expression in the dialogue that means** *(to the) left*.

2 **Find the two examples of the verb poder in the dialogue; can you guess why they are slightly different?**

3 **If vira comes from the verb virar, which verbs do passa and cruza come from?**

1 TRANSLATING *TO THE / AT THE*

The Portuguese word for *to* or *at* (sometimes even *in*) is **a**. Don't confuse it with the feminine word for *the* (which is also **a**). The *to / at* **a** combines with the four words for *the* as follows:

a	+ o	+ a	+ os	+ as
	ao	à	aos	às

ao banco   *to / at the bank*

às minhas amigas   *to my friends*

Don't forget all the other sets of contracted expressions, such as: **do / da** etc; **no / na**, etc; **pelo / pela**, etc!

2 REQUESTING INFORMATION: USING THE VERB **PODER**

Use the expression: **pode me …?** in all kinds of situations requesting assistance:

Pode me …?   *Can you … me?*

indicar   *tell / show*

dizer   *tell*

ajudar   *help*

mostrar   *show*

Don't forget that the form **poderia** is even more polite: *could you …*

3 'EASY' DIRECTIONS USING THE PRESENT TENSE OF VERBS

Use the present tense of verbs, in the **você**, or polite **senhor / senhora**, format, especially to older people, to instruct people what to do:

o senhor vira à esquerda

a senhora cruza a avenida

você toma a primeira à direita

Do the same when speaking to more than one person – use the plural form of the verb:

os senhores viram aqui

as senhoras cruzam o jardim

vocês tomam a segunda rua

Practice 1

1 Complete with ao / à / aos / às.

    a Eu preciso ir _____ farmácia.

    b Manuel vai _____ supermercados.

    c Pamela quer ir _____ praias.

    d Nós vamos _____ museu.

2 Translate – use você in each case.

    a Can you show me on the map?

    b Can you repeat, please?

    c Could you bring (**trazer**) me the menu?

    d Can you help me?

3 What are these instructions telling you to do?

    a Você passa pela praça.

    b Você toma a terceira rua à direita.

    c Você segue em frente.

    d Você sobe aqui.

 4 06.05 Listen to someone asking for help, and place the directions in the order you hear them.

    a turn right

    b cross Augusta avenue

    c carry straight ahead

LANGUAGE TIPS

Some verbs relating to directions have occasional irregular spellings. Note the following:

seguir *(to follow / carry on)* ⟶ **eu sigo**, but **você segue,** etc.

subir *(to go up)* ⟶ **eu subo**, but **você sobe,** etc.

descer *(to go down)* ⟶ **eu desço**, but **você desce,** etc.

Conversation 2

NEW EXPRESSIONS

06.06 Look at the words and expressions that are used in the following conversation. Note their meanings.

devolver estes sapatos	*to return these shoes*
É neste andar?	*Is it on this floor?*
tirar dinheiro	*to withdraw / get money*
um caixa automático	*a cash machine, an ATM*
Pergunte àquela moça.	*Ask that girl.*
Pronto! Chegou.	*There you are!* (lit. *You've arrived*)
É ao lado do café.	*It's next to the café.*
o café Internet é pertinho.	*The Internet café is really near.*

06.07 *Daniel and his friend, Fátima, meet up at the local shopping centre.*
Read and listen to the conversation, then answer the questions.

1 Which floor is the shoe shop on?

Daniel	Oi, Fátima, tudo bem? Então, onde vamos primeiro?
Fátima	Oi Daniel. Bom, primeiro, preciso devolver estes sapatos na sapataria Mariana.
Daniel	Onde é? É neste andar?
Fátima	Não, é no segundo andar. E você, Daniel, o que você quer fazer?
Daniel	Primeiro, tenho que tirar dinheiro. Onde tem um caixa automático aqui dentro?
Fátima	Não tenho certeza. Pergunte àquela moça.
Daniel	Tá. (pause) Desculpe, você sabe onde tem um caixa automático?
Moça	Bom. Você vira aqui à direita, passa em frente do café Internet e pronto, chegou! É ao lado do café.
Daniel	Um momento – então, eu viro à esquerda ….
Moça	Não, à esquerda, não. Vire à direita, e o café Internet é pertinho!
Daniel	Então, tá. Vamos Fátima? E depois vamos ver que filmes estão passando no cinema?

2 Read the conversation again and answer the following questions:
   a Does Fátima know where there's a cash machine?
   b What is the cash machine next to?
   c What else does Daniel suggest they do?

Language discovery 2

1 **If em means** *in*, **and este means** *this*, **can you find the single word in a contracted form in the dialogue which means** *in this*?

2 **In the direction to Daniel to vire à direita, what is different about the word vire compared with how it was used in the first dialogue? Can you guess why?**

3 **What do the contracted expressions ao and do mean in the location of the cash machine – ao lado do café?**

4 **Which expression, from the word for** *near / close* **(perto), means** *really near / close*?

1 *IN / ON THIS* **OR** *THAT*

The word **em** (*in / on*) combines with the words for *this* (**este / esta**) and *that* (**aquele / aquela**), and their plurals as follows:

masc. sing.	fem. sing.	masc. pl.	fem. pl.
neste	nesta	nestes	nestas
naquele	naquela	naqueles	naquelas

nesta loja   *in this shop*

naquele lugar   *in that place*

naquelas paredes   *on those walls*

2 ORDERING PEOPLE TO DO THINGS – THE COMMAND!

To directly order people to do something (or not do something), look at what changes from the ordinary present tense of the verb to make it a direct command:

virar *to turn*   **você vira** *you turn*   **vire!** *turn!*

All regular **-ar** verbs follow this same pattern.

Look at what happens to a regular **-er** or **-ir** verb:

comer *to eat*	**você come** *you eat*	**não coma!** *don't eat!*
abrir *to open*	**você abre** *you open*	**abra!** *open!*

The verb *to go*, **ir**, is as follows:

você vai *you go*   **vá!** *go!*

Be aware, however, that many Brazilians tend to opt for the ordinary present tense version, especially in the spoken language. When listening for directions, just be alert to either variation.

3 EXPRESSING LOCATION: *NEXT TO, BEHIND, ON TOP*, **ETC.**

Common expressions of location include the following:

antes (de)	*before*
ao lado (de)	*next to / by the side of*
até	*up to*
atrás (de)	*behind*
debaixo (de)	*underneath / below*
dentro (de)	*inside*
depois (de)	*after*
em cima (de)	*on top of*
em frente (de)	*in front of / opposite*

In each case, the **de** will combine with relevant words following the expression:

ao lado do banco	*next to the bank*
em cima desta mesa	*on top of this table*
até o fim daquela rua	*up to the end of that road*

o jardim é depois da sapataria?
  Não, é antes.
	Is the garden after the shoe shop?
	  No, it's before.

4 ADDING -INHO TO CHANGE WORDS

Words can change their meaning or emphasis by altering the ending to **-inho/a** or **-zinho/a**. It often makes the expressions softer, smaller, or cuter:

uma casa ⟶ uma casinha	*a little house*
meu irmão ⟶ meu irmãozinho	*my little brother*
uma cerveja ⟶ uma cervejinha	*a nice little beer*
bonito ⟶ bonitinho	*really cute / nice-looking*

Practice 2

1 Complete the text according to the cues.

(In this) **a** _____ cidade, tem muitos lugares para visitar. No centro, *(in these)* **b** _____ ruas, tem bares e restaurantes. *(In that)* **c** _____ praça, tem o Teatro Municipal, e *(in those)* **d** _____ parques você pode relaxar na sombra *(in the shade)*. É muito agradável *(pleasant)*.

2 Correct each statement with a command instruction. Follow the example.

Então, eu viro à direita. ⟶ Não, vire à esquerda!

- **a** Então, eu tomo a primeira rua. ⟶ Não, _____ a segunda rua!
- **b** Então, eu passo por aqui. ⟶ Não, _____ ali!
- **c** Então, eu vou pela praça. ⟶ Não, _____ pelo jardim!
- **d** Então, eu cruzo antes da esquina. ⟶ Não, _____ depois!

3 Guess the meaning and give the original word. For example:

um gatinho ⟶ *a small cat (kitten)* ⟶ um gato

- **a** uma lojinha
- **b** um barzinho
- **c** umas ruazinhas
- **d** uma escolinha

4 06.08 Listen to the description of where places are and indicate on the map what is located at (a), (b), and (c).

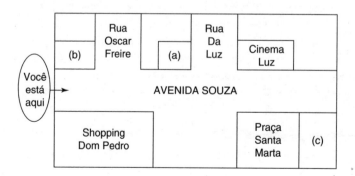

Listen and understand

 06.09 Your Brazilian friend sends you a text message (uma mensagem or um torpedo) with instructions of how to get to her apartment. Listen to the instructions and answer the questions.

    a When should you get off the bus?

    b What should you do soon after getting off the bus?

    c Should you turn left or right to go to Rua Princesa Isabel?

    d What is the number of the building?

    e What is the number of the apartment?

Writing

1 You reply to your friend's message. Choose the correct word for each gap in the text.

| chegar | horas | leva | antes | ponto |

São cinco _____ agora. Estou no _____ de ônibus. A viagem _____ meia hora. Vou _____ na sua casa _____ das seis.

2 06.10 Pronunciation practice

The following words from the conversations all began with **r**: **Recife**, **república**, **repetir**, **rua**. This typically sounds like a hard *h*. Listen to these words again now, with some additional examples, and repeat them, concentrating hard on sounding like the native speaker.

Now listen to how someone from Rio (known as a **Carioca**) will sound the letter **r** when it appears in the middle of or at the end of a word and repeat after the speaker: **voltar**, **viajar**, **parque**, **porque**. That sounds similar to the breathy *ch* in Scottish words such as *loch*. A Brazilian from other areas such as São Paulo or Minas Gerais rolls that **r** more; listen now to how those same words sound; be alert to different pronunciations as you travel around Brazil.

Go further

In banks, post offices, supermarkets, shops and government services buildings you will see a sign for a separate queue, where people with disability or reduced mobility, the elderly, pregnant women and people with babies should go to.

> **PRIORIDADE: PESSOAS COM DEFICIÊNCIA OU MOBILIDADE REDUZIDA, IDOSOS, GESTANTES E PESSOAS COM CRIANÇAS DE COLO.**

You will find these signs inside buildings in Brazil. Can you guess their meaning?

a **SAÍDA DE EMERGÊNCIA**

b **ESTACIONAMENTO NO SUBSOLO**

c **ELEVADORES**

d **CAIXA**

e **PROIBIDO FUMAR**

f **ABERTO**

g **FECHADO**

h **RESTAURANTE NO 3° ANDAR**

Test yourself

1 Which signs do you need to look for?

a you're feeling hungry **1** | CORREIO

b you want to post a letter **2** | CAIXA AUTOMÁTICO

c you need some suncream **3** | LANCHONETE PAULISTA

d you have to buy some groceries **4** | FARMÁCIA LOPES

e you need to get some money **5** | SUPERMERCADO

 2 06.11 Listen to the directions and complete the gaps.

Desculpe, o senhor sabe onde é a **a** _____ Santos?

– Bem, a senhora tem que cruzar esta **b** _____ , virar à **c** _____ , e tomar a **d** _____ rua à esquerda. A farmácia é ao lado do **e** _____ .

3 06.12 Listen and choose the correct number:

a é na 2ª / 6ª rua à esquerda

b é no 4° / 5° andar

c é no 7° / 9° quarteirão

d é na 1ª / 3ª praça à direita

e é na 8ª / 10ª esquina

SELF CHECK

I CAN ...

○ . . . ask where shops and places are.

○ . . . understand basic directions and instructions.

○ . . . request further assistance.

○ . . . find my way around a Brazilian shopping centre.

○ . . . understand expressions of location.

1 Complete with the correct form of comer, beber or conhecer.

   a O Paulo não _____ carne. Ele é vegetariano.
   b Eu não _____ álcool.
   c Nós não _____ a Amazônia.
   d Eles _____ comida italiana todos os sábados.
   e Você _____ uma caipirinha?
   f A Simone _____ muitos restaurantes aqui.

2 6.13 Listen to Mariana speaking about her routine and answer the questions.

   a What time does she get up from Monday to Friday?
   b What does she have for breakfast?
   c When does she have English lessons?
   d What does she do on Sundays?

3 Fill in the gaps with the correct preposition / contraction from the box.

   em   no   na   de

   a O aniversário do Paulo é _____ janeiro.
   b Vamos nos encontrar _____ sexta-feira, _____ restaurante Pitanga?
   c O churrasco vai ser _____ sábado, 10 _____ agosto.
   d _____ domingo _____ tarde eles jogam futebol _____ clube.
   e Nós gostamos _____ ver as novelas _____ televisão.

4 What is he / she doing? Remember to remove the final r from the infinitive of the verb and add -ndo, e.g. falando / comendo / partindo.

a

b

c

d

5 6.14 **Try saying these words out loud, then listen to the correct version.**

> garagem   noite   Rio   Ronaldo
> passaporte   porta   gente   viagem
> bagagem   azeite   restaurante   origem

6 **You are in Rio de Janeiro and want to spend a day in Petrópolis. You go to the ticket office at the rodoviária to enquire about bus times, prices and departure times. Complete your part of the conversation using the cues provided.**

You	*Ask what time there is a bus to Petrópolis.*
Empregado	Há um ônibus de uma em uma hora, a partir das 8 horas da manhã.
You	*Ask how much it costs.*
Empregado	23 reais, só ida.
You	*Ask how long the journey is.*
Empregado	Leva uma hora e quarenta minutos.
You	*Say you want one return ticket.*
Empregado	Aqui está. Boa viagem.

7 6.15 **In Petrópolis, you want to visit the Imperial Museum. You phone the museum and listen to a recorded message about opening times and entrance fees.**
   a Which day of the week is the museum closed?
   b What is the charge for a student?
   c What is the charge for a five-year-old child?

8 **After visiting the Imperial Museum, you decide to go to the Palácio de Cristal (***Crystal Palace***). How would you ask a passer-by:**
   a Do you know where the Palácio de Cristal is?
   b Is the Palácio de Cristal far?
   c Can you show me it on the map?

9 6.16 **You are hungry and ask a passer-by: Há um restaurante aqui perto? Listen to the answer and tick the correct instruction you need to follow.**

10 Do you remember what these signs mean? Match the letters with the English translations.

a	Proibido fumar	_____	Exit
b	Saída	_____	Car Park
c	Caixa	_____	No Smoking
d	Elevador	_____	Closed
e	Estacionamento	_____	Cashier
f	Fechado	_____	Lift

11 6.17 **Listen to the numbers and write them down.**

a _____

b _____

c _____

d _____

e _____

12 Match the item on the left with the shop where you would buy it on the right.

a	livros	**1**	loja de departamentos
b	azeite	**2**	sapataria
c	eletrodomésticos	**3**	feira
d	sandálias	**4**	supermercado
e	frutas	**5**	livraria

13 You ask your friend Guilherme about his plans for the weekend. Complete the questions using a word from the box.

> Onde   Quando   O que
> Como   Quanto tempo

a _____ você vai para Porto Alegre?   Vou no sábado.
b _____ você vai?   Vou de avião.
c _____ você vai ficar em Porto Alegre?   Três dias.
d _____ você vai ficar?   Vou ficar no hotel Continental.
e _____ você vai fazer lá?   Vou no casamento da minha prima.

7 *Temos uma reserva*

We have a reservation

In this unit, you will learn how to:
▶ *discuss your hotel booking.*
▶ *find out about hotel facilities.*
▶ *find your way around a hotel.*
▶ *check opening and meal times.*
▶ *talk about minor problems.*
▶ *complete a typical hotel check-in form.*

CEFR: (A1) *Can pass on personal details in written form;* **(A2)** *Can deal with common aspects of everyday living such as lodgings; Can ask for and provide personal information.*

 ## Alojamento

There are different kinds of **hotéis** (*hotels*) in Brazil. If you want **férias** (*holidays*) with peace and tranquility, you can chill out at a **hotel-fazenda**, generally found in the countryside and featuring large green spaces, walking tracks, horse riding and other sport facilities. There are also many eco-resorts (some self-sustainable) in regions such as the Pantanal, the Amazon and on the island of Fernando de Noronha, where you can enjoy close contact with nature as well as enjoy the many facilities of the property. **Turismo de Aventura** (*adventure tourism*) is becoming very popular, and you can try activities such as rafting or bungee-jumping nearby. Hotels and **pousadas** (*guest houses*) are classified in stars, in line with many parts of the world, **cinco estrelas** (*five stars*) being the best. The word for a room is either **quarto** or **apartamento**, the latter not necessarily being an apartment at all. In general, **café da manhã** is included in the **diária** (*daily rate*) and offers different kinds of **pão**, **bolo**, **queijo e sucos de frutas**, as well as **ovos e bacon**.

It is a good idea to discover when the **época seca e época de chuva** (*dry season and rainy season*) are in each region before you travel.

 If you want to spend a few days in the countryside where you can ride a horse, which kind of accommodation would you look for in Brazil?

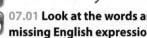# Vocabulary builder

07.01 **Look at the words and phrases and complete the missing English expressions. Then listen and try to imitate the pronunciation of the speakers.**

NO HOTEL	*IN THE HOTEL*
um quarto de casal	*a double room*
um quarto de solteiro	*a single room*
um quarto para família	*a _____ room*
com vista	*with view*
as refeições	*meals*
uma refeição ligeira	*a light _____*
o almoço	*lunch*
a sala de reuniões	*meeting room*
acesso à internet	*Internet _____*

NO QUARTO	*IN THE ROOM*
a cama	*bed*
a toalha	*towel*
o travesseiro	*pillow*
os lençóis	*sheets*
o chuveiro	*shower*
o frigobar	*minibar / fridge*
o ar condicionado	*_____*
o ventilador	*fan*
o cofre	*safe deposit box*
o despertador	*alarm (clock)*

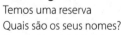**NEW EXPRESSIONS**

07.02 **Look at the words and expressions that are used in the following conversation. Note their meanings.**

Temos uma reserva	*We have a reservation*
Quais são os seus nomes?	*What are your names?*
Como se escreve…?	*How do you spell …? (lit. How is written …?)*
Vocês se importam de preencher esta ficha?	*Do you mind filling in this form?*
A recepção fica aberta	*The reception stays open*
a partir das sete e meia	*from 7.30 onwards*
de manhã cedo	*early in the morning*
de fácil acesso	*easily accessible (lit. of easy access)*

a praia de Encantadas é mais movimentada	the Encantadas beach is busier
Boa estada!	Have a good stay!

Conversation 1

 07.03 *Edward and Susan Towers are checking into the guesthouse Pousada Baleia on the island Ilha do Mel, in southern Brazil, a place known for its ecotourism and tranquillity.*

1 How long is the room booked for?

Edward	Bom dia!
Recepcionista	Bom dia. Pois não?
Edward	Temos uma reserva; um apartamento reservado para oito noites.
Recepcionista	Quais são os seus nomes, por favor?
Edward	Edward e Susan Towers.
Recepcionista	Desculpe, mas como se escreve o seu sobrenome?
Edward	T-O-W-E-R-S: Towers
Recepcionista	Certo. Vocês se importam de preencher esta ficha, por favor? *(pause)* Vocês têm passaportes?
Susan	Aqui.
Recepcionista	Pronto! Esta é a chave do apartamento número vinte e cinco, no segundo andar; a recepção fica aberta vinte e quatro horas por dia.
Susan	A que horas servem o café da manhã?
Recepcionista	Bom, tem café a partir das sete e meia, até as nove horas.
Susan	Que legal! A gente quer ir para a praia de manhã cedo.
Recepcionista	Ah sim – as praias aqui são de fácil acesso; a praia de Fortaleza é deserta, mas a praia de Encantadas é mais movimentada. Boa estada!

2 Read the conversation again and match the questions and answers.

a Quais são os seus nomes?

b Como se escreve o seu sobrenome?

c Vocês têm passaportes?

d A que horas servem o café da manhã?

1 Aqui.

2 T-O-W-E-R-S.

3 Edward e Susan Towers.

4 Tem café a partir das sete e meia.

Vocês se importam de … *Do you mind …* is a more polite version of asking **Vocês poderiam …?** *Could you …?:*

Vocês se importam de assinar aqui / esperar um momento? *Do you mind signing here / waiting a moment?*

Describing places:

calmo	*calm*
tranquilo	*peaceful*
limpo	*clean*
poluído	*polluted*
barulhento	*noisy*

Remember to change the ending to **-a** to describe feminine places: **é uma praia limpa**.

Boa estada! / Boa estadia!	*Have a nice stay!*
Boas férias!	*Enjoy your holidays!*
Boa viagem!	*Have a good journey!*

 # Language discovery 1

1 How are Edward and Susan asked to spell out their surname?

2 Find the plural equivalent of this question in the dialogue: Qual é o seu nome? What has changed?

3 Which verb is used, in its infinitive form, in the time expression from 7.30 (onwards)? What does the verb usually mean?

4 Which three expressions describe the beaches on the island?

1 THE ALPHABET REVISITED

You may well be asked to spell out your name, or part of your address, whilst giving personal information; go back to the audio of the alphabet and tricky sounds from the start of this course and try hard to copy the native speaker's pronunciation. Practise your own names in advance of your visit, and focus particularly on those letters which may have a less familiar sound to you.

2 IRREGULAR PLURALS: L ⟶ IS

Nouns and adjectives ending in **-l** in Portuguese form their plurals as follows:

-al remove **-l** and add **-is** ⟶ **-ais jornal** ⟶ **jornais** *newspapers*

-el remove **-l** and add **-is** ⟶ **-éis papel** ⟶ **papéis** *papers / paperwork*

-ol / -ul remove **-l** and add **-is** ⟶ **-óis / -uis lençol** ⟶ **lençóis**; **azul** ⟶ **azuis**

-il remove **-l** and add **-s** or **-eis** ⟶ **-is / -eis gentil** ⟶ **gentis** *kind*; **difícil** ⟶ **difíceis** *difficult*

Note that some are easier to construct than others depending on the sound of the original word, and may require an additional written accent. Learn them as you go along and make a note of any new ones you find, especially those requiring a written accent.

3 FROM ... UNTIL ...

A partir de ... means *from … (onwards)*, and can be used with all manner of time expressions: **a partir das sete horas**, **a partir da sexta-feira**, **a partir de julho**, etc. To express *up to / until*, use **até**. You will also hear the simple expression **de** (or **do**, etc.) … *from* …: **da uma hora até as duas e trinta**, **do domingo até a terça-feira**, **de março até maio.**

4 ADJECTIVES WITH SER

Don't forget that when using the verb *to be* to describe anything fixed or permanent, use **ser**, and make your adjectives agree with what they are describing in number and gender (masculine or feminine):

as praias são lindas

o hotel é barato

você é engraçado (*funny*)

Practice 1

 1 07.04 Listen to people spelling their surnames and work out what they are.

a _____

b _____

c _____

2 Choose the correct form of each word.

 a O exercício não é fácil / fáceis.

 b Os hotel / hotéis são luxuosos (*luxury*).

 c Estes lençol / lençóis são de algodão (*cotton*).

d Gosto muito do vinho espanhol / espanhóis.

e A água é azul / azuis turquesa (*turquoise*).

3 Give the English for the following time expressions.

a There is breakfast from 7 o'clock (onwards).

b There's music (**música**) from Thursday to Saturday.

c They serve lunch from midday until 2.30.

d From November onwards there are many visitors (**visitantes**).

4 Complete with the correct adjective.

> pequenos movimentada
> feias (*ugly*) inteligente

a A cidade é _____.

b Os apartamentos são _____.

c João é _____.

d As praias são _____.

Conversation 2

NEW EXPRESSIONS

07.05 Look at the words and expressions that are used in the following conversation. Note their meanings.

Desculpe incomodar	*Excuse me interrupting*
acabo de chegar	*I have just arrived*
a convenção sobre biodiversidade	*the conference about biodiversity.*
Falta um livrinho de informações	*There's an information booklet missing*
para o uso exclusivo dos nossos hóspedes	*for the exclusive use of our guests*
Aliás	*What is more / Moreover*
Quais são as horas de abertura?	*What are the opening times?*
está suja e precisamos limpar	*it's dirty and we need to clean it*
a qualquer hora	*at any time*

07.06 *Argentinian businesswoman Edith García is checking out the facilities at the hotel where her conference is being held.*

1 Which room is Edith looking for?

Edith	Boa tarde! Desculpe incomodar – acabo de chegar e queria me informar sobre as facilidades do hotel.
Recepcionista	Com certeza. A senhora está aqui para a convenção sobre biodiversidade?
Edith	Estou, sim. Onde fica a sala de reuniões? Falta um livrinho de informações no quarto.
Recepcionista	Um momento, sim? *(calls to colleague)* – Marta, vou orientar a senhora García por dez minutos, tá?
Marta	Tudo bem, Francisco.
Recepcionista	*(slowly)* Então, aqui, à esquerda, tem a sala de convenções, com mais quatro salas de reuniões ao lado. Ao fim do corredor, no canto, tem escritório com computadores para o uso exclusivo dos nossos hóspedes. Aliás, todos os quartos têm acesso à internet.
Edith	Ótimo!

 07.07 *The tour of the hotel continues.*

2 What are the opening times of the hotel gym?

Recepcionista	Depois, temos nossa academia no subsolo do hotel; tem piscina, jacuzzi, sauna, tudo.
Edith	Quais são as horas de abertura?
Recepcionista	Geralmente, abre a partir das seis da manhã, e fecha às vinte e três horas. Hoje a sauna está fechada porque está suja e precisamos limpar.
Edith	E a que horas são as refeições?
Recepcionista	O restaurante abre às seis e trinta para o café da manhã. Também serve almoço e jantar, mas também pode comer refeições ligeiras no bar a qualquer hora.

3 Read, then listen to, the whole conversation again and answer the questions.

   a Is the conference room on the left or the right?
   b Where is the hotel gym located?
   c Why is the sauna closed today?
   d When can you eat light meals in the bar?

LANGUAGE TIPS

More prepositions:

no canto	*in the corner*
ao fim de / no fim de	*at the end of*

You can express what's not working properly in your room by using **não funciona / funcionam** *it doesn't work / they don't work*:

a torneira não funciona	*the tap doesn't work*

 # Language discovery 2

1 In the expression for *I have just arrived*, **which verb means** *to arrive*? **What verb does acabo come from?**

2 What is the word order in Portuguese for the phrase *there's a booklet missing*?

3 If convenções is the plural of convenção, what is the singular of reuniões?

4 Which two adjectives describe the current state of the hotel sauna?

1 ACABAR DE … *TO HAVE JUST …*

To express an action that has just taken place, use the present tense of the verb **acabar**, followed by **de**, then the action in the infinitive form of the verb:

acabo de jantar	*I've just had dinner*
ela acaba de partir	*she's just left*
acaba de chover	*it's just rained*

2 FALTAR *TO BE MISSING / LACKING*

Faltar could be described as a sort of back-to-front verb, as you follow it by the item or items that are missing. Use it in the third person singular or plural forms:

Falta uma toalha; **falta leite**; **faltam dois garfos** (*forks*); **faltam pratos**

You may also hear the expression **há / tem uma falta de ...** *there's a lack of ...*:

há uma falta de educação   *there's a lack of good manners*

3 IRREGULAR PLURALS: ÃO

Nouns and adjectives ending in **-ão** in Portuguese form their plurals in the following ways – but there are no hard and fast rules about which form any particular word takes; you need to learn new plurals as you come across them:

ão ⟶ ões (the most common) OR ⟶ **ães** ⟶ OR ⟶ **ãos**

estação ⟶ estações   **pão ⟶ pães** **mão ⟶ mãos**

4 ADJECTIVES WITH ESTAR

When using *to be* to describe anything temporary or not fixed, such as weather, emotions, state of health, situations that can change or have changed, use the verb **estar** with adjectives, remembering to make those agree with the nouns in question:

a banheira não está limpa   *the bathtub isn't clean*

todos os museus estão   *all the museums are closed today*
  fechados hoje

 Practice 2

1 Match the expressions to the pictures to say what has just happened.

a

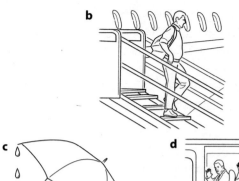

1 acaba de chover
2 acabam de partir
3 acabamos de jantar
4 acabo de chegar

 2 **07.08 Listen and decide what's missing.**

a _____
b _____
c _____
d _____
e _____

3 **Find the word that doesn't match the ending pattern. Then decide what the singular of that word is.**

a	alemães	aviões	pães	capitães (*captains*)
b	irmãos	mãos	estações	grãos (*grains*)
c	porções	atrações	televisões	órgãos (*organs*)

4 **Complete with the correct part of estar from the first line in the box and an appropriate adjective from the next two lines.**

> estão está estou estamos
> tristes (*sad*) cansada (*tired*)
> abertas frio

a Eu (f.) _____ _____.

b Hoje o tempo (*weather*) _____ muito _____.

c As lojas não _____ _____ hoje.

d Nós _____ _____.

Reading and listening

William reads an advert for a hotel in Ilhabela, on the coast of the state of São Paulo.

Read the advert and answer the questions.

rodeado por	*surrounded by*
relaxante	*relaxing*
paisagem	*countryside*

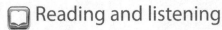

Hotel Itapemar em Ilhabela - rodeado por muito verde e uma paisagem linda e relaxante. Um local perfeito para passeios a pé e de bicicleta. A praia fica pertinho! São sessenta apartamentos grandes, confortáveis e bem equipados. O restaurante serve pratos deliciosos de peixe. A área de lazer inclui sauna, quadras de squash e tênis.

1 What is the location perfect for?

2 How many rooms are there?

3 What dishes might tempt you in the restaurant?

4 What leisure activities can you participate in?

07.09 *William decides to go to Ilhabela and makes a reservation at the Hotel Itapemar. He is in the city of São Paulo at the moment.*

Listen to the dialogue and answer the questions.

balsa	*a barge or ferry that transports people and vehicles*

5 How can William get to Ilhabela from São Paulo?
   a by bus or car and then on foot
   b by boat and then by car
   c by bus or car and then by boat

6 How long will it take to get to Ilhabela, from São Sebastião?
   a 15 minutes
   b half an hour
   c an hour

7 How often do the barges leave for Ilhabela?
   a once a day
   b twice a day
   c many times a day

8 07.10 **Pronunciation practice**

The word for *underground* is spelled **S-U-B-S-O-L-O**, but many Brazilians say it as though there were an **I** after the **B**. Listen to that word again now. Try picturing the spelling of the word and then its pronunciation as you say it. Other examples of where an extra vowel is often added when speaking include: **absurdo** *absurd* (sounds like **abisurdo**), **Magda** (sounds like **Máguida**) and **ritmo** *rhythm* (sounds like **ritimo**). There is further guidance on this in the **Pronunciation guide** at the start of the course.

Reading

Sonia writes a feedback form to management of the hotel where she stayed in São Paulo:

> O hotel é muito velho. O quarto precisa de uma televisão nova. O acesso à internet não está incluído no preço da diária, uma grande inconveniência. As cortinas estão sujas e o chuveiro é ruim. Não é um hotel de três estrelas, mas de duas estrelas! Fiquei decepcionada (I was disappointed).

What does Sonia say is wrong in the room? Find the correct answer in the second column.

a	hotel and TV	**1**	dirty
b	shower	**2**	not included in the price
c	Internet access	**3**	old
d	curtains	**4**	rubbish

Go further

Look at the hotel check-in form that William had to fill in when he arrived in Ilhabela.

Ficha de registro de entrada no hotel	
Nome: *William*	Sobrenome: *Slater*
Data de nascimento *10/05/1963*	Local de nascimento: *York, Inglaterra*
Número da Identidade / passaporte: *900352803*	
Endereço: *305 Whitestone Street, Kendal LA9 Inglaterra*	

data de nascimento	*date of birth*
local de nascimento	*place of birth*
número da identidade / passaporte	*identity card / passport number*
endereço	*address*

The date 10/05/1963 means day/month/year.

Now complete the form with your own details.

Ficha de registro de entrada no hotel	
Nome:	Sobrenome:
Data de nascimento:	Local de nascimento:
Número da Identidade / passaporte:	
Endereço:	

Test yourself

1 Rearrange the words into complete sentences.

  a informar praias sobre me as Queria.

  b do a reuniões corredor de tem sala Ao fim.

  c as abertura horas são de Quais?

  d no qualquer comer hora a Pode bar.

2 07.11 Listen to the conversation and complete with the missing information in Portuguese.

  a Tipo de quarto? _____

  b Para quantas noites? _____

  c Sobrenome? _____

  d Número do quarto? _____

3 Have a go at saying these out loud in Portuguese.

  a I have a reservation.

  b We have a room booked for five nights.

  c What time is breakfast served?

  d Does the room have a safe deposit box?

SELF CHECK

I CAN ...
... discuss my hotel booking.
... find out about hotel facilities.
... find my way around a hotel.
... check opening and meal times.
... talk about minor problems.
... complete a typical hotel check-in form.

8 Pois não?

Can I help you?

In this unit, you will learn how to:
▶ *ask for clothing and other items by colour and size.*
▶ *understand and react to recommendations and suggestions.*
▶ *specify this, that, these and those.*
▶ *request information about products.*
▶ *understand numbers above 1,000.*

CEFR: (A1) *Can ask people for things; Can handle numbers and quantities;* **(A2)** *Can make simple purchases by stating what is wanted and asking the price.*

Fazendo compras

Many Brazilians like to do their weekly or monthly shopping in hypermarkets such as Extra, Carrefour, Walmart and Makro, where they can buy everything and there is **estacionamento grátis** (*free parking*). Some cities and towns have designated shopping streets with a large concentration of small shops selling all kinds of products at big discounts. Middle-class Brazilians in particular are almost addicted to shopping malls, referred to as **o shopping**, and also love to visit **lojas de departamentos** (*department stores*). Fun shopping can also be had at local **feirinhas** (*markets* – mostly for fresh food) and the **feira hippy** (*artisan market*). If you are in search of bargains, look for signs saying **LIQUIDAÇÃO** (*sale*) and **DESCONTOS** (*discounts*). In general, you can buy **roupas** (*clothes*), **sapatos** (*shoes*) and **móveis** (*furniture*) **à vista** (*paid there and then*) or **à prazo e sem juros** (*paid in interest-free instalments*).

 What does this sign mean?

LIQUIDAÇÃO 40% de desconto nas compras à vista e a prazo.

V Vocabulary builder

08.01 Look at the words and phrases and complete the missing English expressions. Then listen and try to imitate the pronunciation of the speakers.

ROUPA(S)	*CLOTHING / CLOTHES*
a blusa	_____
a saia	*skirt*
a calça	*trousers*
o vestido	*dress*
a camiseta	*T-shirt*
a camisa	*shirt*
o terno	*suit (men's)*
a gravata	*tie*
os tênis	*trainers*
as sandálias	_____
o short	*shorts*

LANGUAGE TIP
The words for *trousers* and *shorts* are singular in Portuguese. **Tênis** can also be singular when it refers to one trainer and the singular forms of **sandálias** and **sapatos** are **sandália** and **sapato** respectively.

CORES	*COLOURS*
preto	*black*
branco	_____
amarelo	*yellow*
vermelho	*red*
roxo	*purple*
azul	*blue*
verde	_____
laranja	*orange*
marrom	*brown*
cinza	*grey*
(cor-de-)rosa	*pink*
bege	_____

NEW EXPRESSIONS

08.02 **Look at the words and expressions that are used in the following conversation. Note their meanings.**

talvez de seda, com manga comprida	*perhaps (made of) silk, with short sleeves*
no tamanho	*in size*
são de linho	*they're (made of) linen*
São as mais bonitas da loja.	*They're the prettiest in the shop.*
deixe ver	*let me see*
temos aquelas ali	*we have those over there*
essa que você tem aí	*that one that you have there*
À vontade.	*Of course / As you wish.*
o provador	*the changing room*
combina bem	*it goes well*

Conversation 1

08.03 *Rodrigo has gone shopping with his friend Vanda, who wants a new blouse.*

1 What colour of blouse is Vanda looking for?

Rodrigo	Vanda, que tipo de blusa você está procurando?
Vanda	Talvez de seda, com manga comprida, sei lá, Rodrigo, depende do preço.
(The shop assistant approaches.)	
Empregada	Pois não, senhora?
Vanda	Boa tarde. Estou procurando uma blusa preta; o que vocês têm no tamanho quarenta?
Empregada	Bom, temos estas aqui, que são de linho – muito confortáveis.
Vanda	Quanto custam?
Empregada	Sessenta e cinco reais cada. São as mais bonitas da loja.
Vanda	Hmm, um pouco cara para mim. Não tem mais barata?
Empregada	Mais barata, hmm, deixe ver – temos aquelas ali de algodão em várias cores.
Vanda	Posso experimentar essa que você tem aí?
Empregada	À vontade. O provador é ali, à esquerda.
(Five minutes later)	

| **Vanda** | Então, Rodrigo, o que você acha? |
| **Rodrigo** | Nossa Vanda, que linda! Fica muito bem em você. Acho que combina bem com a sua saia. |

2 **Read the conversation again and, with the help of the new expressions, answer the questions.**
   a What is the price of the linen blouses?
   b Where is the changing room located?
   c According to Rodrigo, what does the blouse go well with?

 3 **Now listen to the conversation again, repeating after each line, and concentrating on your pronunciation.**

> **INSIGHT**
>
> Clothing sizes in Brazil follow European sizes, or are expressed as: **pequeno (P)**, **médio (M)**, **grande (G)** and **extra grande (GG)**. Shoes also follow European sizes. It's always best to try first, however, as Brazilian sizes can often be smaller than elsewhere.
>
> | **fica / ficam bem** | *it suits / they suit you* |
> | **serve / servem** | *it fits / they fit* |
> | **combina / combinam com …** | *it goes / they go with …* |
> | **está apertado/a** | *it's tight* |
> | **manga comprida / curta** | *long- / short-sleeved* |
> | **de veludo / jeans / cetim / couro / lã** | *(made of) velvet / denim / satin / leather / wool* |
> | **xadrez** | *checked* |
> | **listrado** | *striped* |
> | **florido** | *flowery* |

💡 Language discovery 1

1 **Find the expression for a black blouse. How do you think you say** *a white blouse***?**

2 **What is the opposite of estas aqui?**

3 **Find the Portuguese for a)** *expensive* **b)** *cheaper* **(i.e.** *more cheap***) c)** *the prettiest* **(i.e.** *the most pretty***). Why are the adjectives all in the feminine?**

1 ADJECTIVES OF COLOUR

Colours ending in **-o** have four different forms depending on gender and number:

preto → preta / pretos / pretas

uma blusa preta

os sapatos pretos

Those ending in **-e** or a consonant only have one singular and one plural form:

verde → **verdes**

azul → **azuis**

marrom → **marrons**

uma camisa azul

meias (*socks*) **marrons**

Colours such as **cinza**, **laranja** and **(cor-de-)rosa** don't change at all:

um biquíni laranja

os maiôs (*swimming costumes*) **cor-de-rosa**

If you're unsure, you can express a colour in its masculine singular form, preceding it by **em** (*in*):

uma sunga (*swimming trunks*) **em cinza**

You can also use **-escuro** (*dark*) and **-claro** (*light*):

uma saia verde-escura

um chapéu (*hat*) **em roxo-claro**

2 THIS AND THAT; HERE AND THERE

	masc. sing.	masc. pl.	fem. sing.	fem. pl.	
aqui (*here*)	este	estes	esta	estas	*this / these*
aí (*there*)	esse	esses	essa	essas	*that / those*
ali (*over there*)	aquele	aqueles	aquela	aquelas	*that / those*

You should use **esse**, etc. when referring to something near to the person you're talking to (i.e. that thing you have there). For anything at a distance from both parties, use **aquele**, etc.

Este bolo é bom. Esses bolos que você tem aí são melhores. Aqueles bolos ali são os meus favoritos.	*This cake is good. Those cakes you have there are better. Those cakes over there are my favourites.*

In practice, however, Brazilians don't pay much attention to the rules! You will come across **aí** and **ali** used interchangeably as well as **lá** for *over there*, far from the speaker. Be prepared for anything!

3 CHEAP, CHEAPER, CHEAPEST

To compare things using adjectives, use **mais** (*more*) and the correct
form of the adjective: **esta calça é mais barata** *these trousers are cheaper*
(lit. *more cheap*); to express the extreme, or superlative, form of an
adjective, place the relevant word for *the* in front of **mais**: **são os mais
confortáveis** (*they are the most comfortable*). Note the following word
order: **é a jaqueta mais cara da loja**: *it's the most expensive jacket in the
shop* (lit. *it's the jacket more expensive of the shop*)

 Practice 1

1 Complete by forming the colour correctly.
   a um prato (*green*)
   b três bicicletas (*yellow*)
   c dois carros (*brown*)
   d uma ameixa (*plum*) (*purple*)

2 Express what is in the images using *this* **and** *that,* **etc., and** *here*
   and *there,* **following this example:**

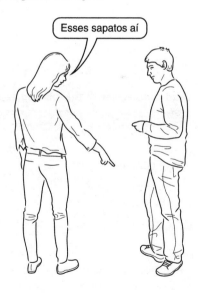

Esses sapatos aí

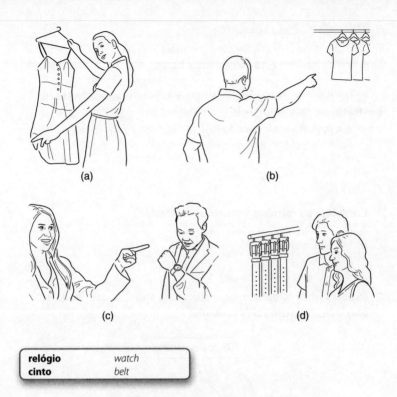

(a) (b)

(c) (d)

| relógio | watch |
| cinto | belt |

3 08.04 Listen and complete with the missing expressions.

> fresca   o mais   nova   mais

Eu gosto muito de roupa _____. No verão uso roupa de algodão, que é
mais _____. No inverno (*in winter*), prefiro roupa _____ quente; adoro
meu vestido de lã – é _____ lindo que tenho!

Conversation 2

 NEW EXPRESSIONS

 08.05 Look at the words and expressions that are used in the following conversation. Note their meanings.

né?	*aren't they? / isn't it? / eh?*
Tem as havaianas em promoção.	*The flip-flops are on special offer.*
Vou levar um par.	*I'm going to take a pair.*
Combina melhor com a sua bolsa!	*It goes better with your bag!*
Estão na moda.	*They're in fashion.*
Me dá essa listrada.	*Give me that striped one.*
Estou à procura de …	*I'm looking for …*
música sertaneja	*country music*
Estão todos na oferta	*They're all on offer*
O que é isso?	*What's that?*
A variedade é enorme.	*There is a huge variety. (lit. The variety is huge.)*
o mais vendido do verão	*the bestseller of the summer (lit. the most sold of the summer)*
já venderam	*they've already sold*

 08.06 *Lara is chatting with a stallholder at the feira hippy in Recife.*

1   What does Lara buy a pair of, and in what colour?

Lara	Oi, tudo bem? Que coisas mais bonitas você tem!
Vendedor	São lindíssimas, né? Hoje, menina, tem as havaianas em promoção - olha que desenhos maravilhosos!
Lara	Gosto muito destas aqui em laranja e azul. Vou levar um par – número trinta e seis, por favor. Ah, você também tem toalhas de praia, ótimo!
Vendedor	Que tal aquela? Combina melhor com a sua bolsa!
Lara	Tudo bem. Que mais você tem?
Vendedor	Estas bandanas estão na moda no momento.
Lara	Me dá essa listrada que você tem aí. Obrigada.

Meanwhile, David has come across a stall selling CDs.

2 What does MPB stand for?

Vendedora	Você precisa de ajuda?
David	Oi! Estou à procura de música típica do Brasil. O que você sugere?
Vendedora	Tem estes CDs de bossa nova, de samba, de música sertaneja, e estes são de MPB. Estão todos na oferta, com preços baratíssimos.
David	MPB – o que é isso?
Vendedora	Música Popular Brasileira – todo mundo gosta! A variedade é enorme.
David	E aquele, o que é?
Vendedora	Este grupo é novo, mas o disco é o mais vendido do verão, já venderam mais de 25 mil CDs; é um ritmo típico do nordeste – se chama forró.
David	Então, dê-me esses três por favor. Obrigado pela ajuda.

3 Read the conversations again and answer True or False.

  a The most fashionable products at the moment are plastic belts.
  b David is shown three different types of CD.
  c The best-selling CD of the summer is by an new group.

 # Language discovery 2

1 Find the expressions meaning the same as: muito lindas / muito baratos.

2 What's the expression for How about … ? / What about …?

3 How many CDs have the best-selling group sold? How might you say 48 thousand?

4 Which two expressions both mean give me?

1 -ÍSSIMO *VERY …*

A nice alternative to using **muito** + adjective (*very / really* …) is to add **-íssimo/a** to the end of the adjective. For the majority of adjectives (ending in **-o** or **-e**), remove the last letter and add **-íssimo/a** instead (remembering to use the correct ending depending on whether the noun in question is masculine or feminine):

lindo ⟶ **lindíssimo: a minha irmã é lindíssima**

inteligente ⟶ **inteligentíssimo: os estudantes são inteligentíssimos**

Note that **ótimo** is used to mean **muito bom** and **péssimo** to mean **muito mau**:

Esta revista é péssima!　　　*This magazine is awful!*

2 RECOMMENDING, SUGGESTING AND REQUESTING ADVICE

O que você sugere / recomenda / acha / aconselha? *What do you suggest / recommend / think / advise?*

Que tal …?	*What / How about …?*
Por que não …?	*Why not …?*
Por que não compra o azul?	*Why don't you buy the blue one?*

You can reply using **Você tem razão** *You're right*; **(Não) concordo com você** *I (don't) agree with you*.

3 NUMBERS GREATER THAN 1,000 – AN OVERVIEW

The word for *one thousand* (**mil**) never changes its form: **dois mil**, **quarenta mil**, **setecentos mil**. Portuguese uses a full stop in written numbers where in English a comma would be used: **1.567** *1,567*; **38.900** *38,900*. Years are expressed as a full number, e.g. 1985 = **mil, novecentos e oitenta e cinco**. You should apply the previous rules for forming the hundreds and tens, including feminine forms. The joining word **e** (*and*) is used after the thousand only when the thousand is followed directly by a number from 1 to 100, e.g. 2,065 = **dois mil e sessenta e cinco**, or when the thousand is followed by a number ending in 00, e.g. 16,800 = **dezesseis mil e oitocentos**.

4 ME DÁ / DÊ-ME *GIVE ME*

The grammatically correct way to say *give me* is **dê-me**; however, what you hear much of the time is the more casual **me dá**. Other examples of a more relaxed approach to the rules include: **me mostra** instead of **mostre-me** (*show me*), **me telefona** instead of **telefone-me** (*phone me*), **me manda uma mensagem / um email** instead of **mande-me …** (*send me a message / an email*), **me conta** instead of **me conte** (*tell me*). Remember that many languages have different formal and informal words and constructions – just be alert to different forms as you listen.

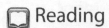 Practice 2

1 Complete with the correct form of the adjective ending in -íssimo.

a O seu gato é (gordo) (*fat*) _____.
b Estas camisas são (baratas) _____.
c Que decisão (muito boa) _____!
d O novo filme é (muito chato) (*awful / boring*) _____.
e Os bilhetes são (muito caros) _____.

2 08.07 Listen and note down in English what is recommended or suggested.

a _____.
b _____.
c _____.

3 08.08 Listen and choose the correct number in each case.

a	2.518	2.508	25.518
b	1974	1965	1975
c	36.004	36.400	36.014
d	1.089	1.088	11.089
e	72.262	62.462	72.462

4 Convert the underlined verbs in Amélia's message to Mariana from formal to informal forms.

> Oi Mariana! Tudo bem?
>
> Amiga, <u>telefone-me</u> ou (*or*) <u>mande-me</u> um email porque (*because*) quero saber suas notícias (*news*). <u>Conte-me</u> tudo!
>
> Um beijo (*a kiss*),
>
> Amélia x

Reading

NA LOJA DE DEPARTAMENTOS

1 Try to guess which department of the store you would visit to buy the following items.

116

1. → Moda

2. → Perfumaria

3. → Esportes

4. → Aparelhos elétricos & eletrônicos

5. → Eletrodomésticos

6. → Casa (móveis e têxteis)

7. → Alimentação

8. → Cultura e Lazer

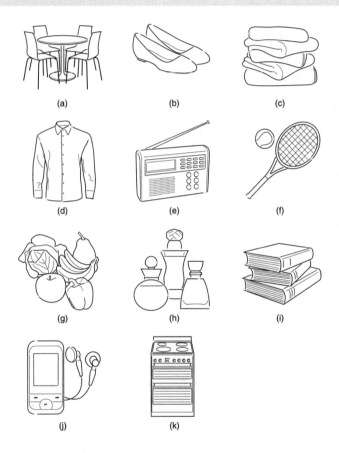

(a) (b) (c)

(d) (e) (f)

(g) (h) (i)

(j) (k)

2 08.09 Pronunciation practice

The letter **x** in Portuguese has different sounds, but it's not always easy to decide which way to pronounce it when you first come across new words, as the rules are not rigid. You need to note down the spelling and sound of the words as you discover them. Listen now to two words you heard in the dialogues: the expression for *let me see* (**deixe ver**) and the verb *to try on* (**experimentar**) – the letter **x** is pronounced differently in each one. Listen to the audio and practise some more examples.

Go further

Na loja *in the shop*. Read the following important phrases and practise saying them out loud.

Posso ver …?	*Can I see …?*
Posso provar / experimentar?	*Can I try it on?*
Prefiro este / esta.	*I prefer this one.*
É muito pequeno(a) / grande (a).	*It's too small / big.*
Tem menor?	*Do you have a smaller size?*
Tem maior?	*Do you have a larger size?*
É muito curto(a) / longo(a).	*It's very short / long.*
Não gosto da cor / do estilo.	*I don't like the colour / the style.*
Estou só vendo.	*I'm only looking.*

Listen and understand

08.10 Listen to Jorge buying a shirt and answer the questions:

1 **What style of shirt is he looking for?**
2 **What is his size?**
3 **Which colour does he prefer?**

 ## Speaking

Let's practise! Now it's your turn to ask for help in a shop. Fill in the gaps and say your part of the dialogue out loud.

Empregada	Quer ajuda?
You	Tem … / Queria … / Posso ver… *(say what you want)*?
Empregada	Que tamanho?
You	Pequeno / Médio / Grande / GG or 42, 44, 46, 48, etc.
Empregada	Que cor prefere?
You	Prefiro … *(say which colour you prefer)*
Shop assistant	Mais alguma coisa?
You	Não, isso é tudo. Obrigado(a).

Test yourself

1 Follow the clues to find the clothing or accessories.

   a roupa feminina para a praia B _ _ _ _ _ _

   b para saber as horas, precisa dum R _ _ _ _ _ _

   c se usam nos pés S _ _ _ _ _ _

   d roupa masculina formal T _ _ _ _

   e para uma festa *(party)*, um … elegante V _ _ _ _ _ _

2 08.11 Listen and decide if each statement is True or False.

   a He's looking for a brown jacket.

   b She likes Paulo's green flip-flops.

   c He only has hats in red or purple.

   d She suggests new bags in yellow or white.

SELF CHECK

	I CAN ...
○	... ask for clothing and other items by colour and size.
○	... understand and react to recommendations and suggestions.
○	... specify *this*, *that*, *these* and *those*.
○	... request information about products.
○	... understand numbers above 1,000.

9 *Planos para o feriado*

Plans for the bank holiday

In this unit, you will learn how to:
▶ *talk about future plans.*
▶ *say what you would like to do.*
▶ *accept or decline invitations.*
▶ *recognize typical Brazilian celebrations.*
▶ *discuss typical holiday activities.*

CEFR: (A2) *Can describe plans and arrangements; Can make and respond to invitations, suggestions and apologies; Can understand short, simple personal letters or messages.*

 Celebrações

Festas de aniversário de crianças (*children's birthday parties*) can be **eventos grandes** (*large events*), and also **muito caros**. Not only are children invited, but so are **a família toda**, **os vizinhos** (*the neighbours*) **e os amigos**, easily reaching more than 100 **convidados** (*guests*)! A *special venue* (**um salão de festa**) is sometimes hired to fit everyone in and to keep the kids entertained. **Batizados** (*christenings*) are important family occasions that bring relatives and friends together. When a girl reaches 15, the occasion can be marked with a formal celebration called **Festa de Quinze Anos** (*fifteenth birthday party*) or she can join a **Baile das Debutantes**, a formally organized celebration for many girls at the same time, marking the transition from childhood to young womanhood. Many families cannot afford to do this, and the occasion is marked with **um presente especial**, **uma viagem** or **uma reunião de família**. **Casamentos** (*weddings*) are very big affairs, and most take place in the evening. A large reception follows a church ceremony. In most receptions, finger food is served with cake and champagne at the end, instead of a sit-down meal, as the number of guests can easily go beyond 200!

 What have you been invited to if you receive an invitation to a **batizado**, **aniversário**, **festa de quinze anos** or **casamento**?

Vocabulary builder

 09.01 Look at the words and phrases and complete the missing English expressions. Then listen and try to imitate the pronunciation of the speakers.

FÉRIAS, FERIADOS E CELEBRAÇÕES	*HOLIDAYS, BANK HOLIDAYS AND CELEBRATIONS*
as Festas Juninas	*'June' festivals (celebrating Saints Antônio, João and Pedro)*
o Natal	*Christmas*
o Reveillon	*New Year's Eve*
a Páscoa	*Easter*
a Semana Santa	*Holy _____*
o Carnaval	*_____*
o feriado	*bank holiday*
o Dia da Independência	*_____ Day (7 September)*
o Dia da Proclamação da República	*Day of the Proclamation of the Republic (15 November)*

ATIVIDADES	*ACTIVITIES*
ir ao clube	*to go to the club*
fazer um churrasco	*to have a barbecue*
visitar a família	*_____*
ir para a praia	*to go to the beach*
viajar	*to travel*
ir pescar	*to go fishing*
ir pro (= para o) interior / litoral	*to go to the country / to the coast*
fazer uma trilha	*to go hiking*

 NEW EXPRESSIONS

 09.02 Look at the words and expressions that are used in the following conversation. Note their meanings.

Tô (= Estou) pensando em visitar	*I'm thinking about visiting*
Estávamos pensando	*We were thinking*
Você quer ir conosco?	*Do you want to go with us?*
seria ótimo, mas não tem jeito	*it would be great, but it won't work / won't be possible*
o feriado inteirinho	*the whole bank holiday*
na fazenda	*on the farm / family estate*

sobrinho	*nephew*
pipoca	*popcorn*
amendoim torrado	*roasted peanut(s)*
um montão de coisas	*a pile of things*
fim de semana	*weekend*

Conversation 1

09.03 *Colleagues Sebastião and Irene are discussing their plans for the bank holiday.*

1 How were Sebastião and his family planning on spending the bank holiday?

Sebastião	Então, Irene, você tem planos para o feriado?
Irene	Tô pensando em visitar minha família no interior. E você, Sebastião?
Sebastião	Não sei exatamente. Estávamos pensando em passar umas horinhas no clube. Meus filhos adoram ficar na piscina.
Irene	Quem não gosta?
Sebastião	Você quer ir conosco?
Irene	Ah, Sebastião, seria ótimo, mas não tem jeito. Vou passar o feriado inteirinho na fazenda; tem o batizado do meu sobrinho.
Sebastião	Ah é? Vocês vão fazer churrasco?
Irene	Vamos sim, e as crianças querem pipoca, amendoim torrado, um montão de coisas, sabe?
Sebastião	Tá. Então por que não vem com a gente no próximo fim de semana?
Irene	Tudo bem, Sebastião. Obrigadíssima pelo convite!

2 Read the conversation again, and with the help of the new expressions, answer the questions.
   a What do Sebastião's children love doing?
   b What event is Irene's family celebrating?
   c When does Sebastião suggest that Irene goes with them to the club?

3 Now listen to the dialogue again, pausing the audio and repeating after each line, concentrating hard on sounding like the native speakers.

💡 Language discovery 1

1 **Which expressions mean** *I am thinking* **and** *We were thinking*? **Which two Portuguese verbs are used in each case?**

2 **Find two different ways of expressing** *with us*; **which is formal and which is informal?**

3 **The word montão comes from the word for** *hill* **(monte); what effect does the -ão ending give it?**

4 **Find the singular form of these words: fins de semana, amendoins.**

1 I AM / I WAS THINKING OF DOING

An action going on at the moment is expressed by taking the present tense of **estar** + the verb in its **-ando / -endo / -indo** format. **Pensar + em** + the verb in the infinitive means *to think of / about …ing*:

Estamos pensando em comprar uma casa. *We're thinking of buying a house.*

To express the same idea in the past (*was / were thinking of …*), use **estar** in the following forms:

eu estava	**nós estávamos**
ele / ela / você estava	**eles / elas / vocês estavam**

Eles estavam pensando em passar o Natal em São Paulo.	*They were thinking of spending Christmas in São Paulo.*

2 PRONOUNS WITH COM

Com a gente is the colloquial way to say *with us*; the more standard way is **conosco**; similarly **comigo** means *with me*. For all other *with* expressions (*with him*, *with her*, etc.), use **com** + subject pronouns: **com ele**, **com ela**, **com você**, **com eles**, and so on. You will also hear **contigo**, meaning *with you*, often in song lyrics.

Eu vou com vocês.	*I'm going / I go with you.*
Ela não quer ir com eles.	*She doesn't want to go with them.*

3 UM MONTÃO – THE ENDING -ÃO

By using **-ão** to alter the end of words, you can create the effect of something appearing *larger*, *grander*, *stronger*, *uglier*, etc. Typical examples include:

carta *letter* ⟶ **cartão** *card / cardboard*

porta *door* ⟶ **portão** *gate*

sala *room* ⟶ **salão** *hall / ballroom*

Usually the original feminine gender of a word changes to masculine.

4 IRREGULAR PLURALS: M ⟶ NS

Nouns and adjectives ending in **-m** form their plural by changing the **-m** to **-ns**:

homem *man* ⟶ **homens** *men*

viagem ⟶ **viagens**

comum *common* ⟶ **comuns**

 Practice 1

1 Match the Portuguese and English.

a Estou pensando em trabalhar amanhã.

b Estavam pensando em vender o carro.

c Ela estava pensando em visitar o amigo.

d Você está pensando em sair no sábado?

e O que você estava pensando em fazer?

1 She was thinking of visiting her friend.

2 What were you thinking of doing?

3 I'm thinking of working tomorrow.

4 They were thinking about selling the car.

5 Are you thinking of going out on Saturday?

 **2 09.04 Listen and select what you hear.**

a Mônica quer sair com eles / com você.

b João, você vem conosco / comigo?

c Eles não podem ir com a gente / com ela.

d Posso ir com ele / contigo?

3 Replace the words in italics with a word or expression from the box.

gatão	cachorrão	um tempão
beijão	abração	um garrafão

a Paula tem um *gato enorme*.
b Estamos esperando o ônibus *por muito tempo*.
c Temos sede; precisamos comprar *uma garrafa gigante* de água.
d A Joana tem um *cachorro enorme* chamado Tufão.
e Um *beijo grande* pra (= para a) tia Cecília.
f Um *abraço grande* pra você.

4 Add the missing singular or plural forms.

Singular	Plural
jardim	
mensagem	
	sons (*sounds*)
bombom (*sweet*)	
	nuvens (*clouds*)

Conversation 2

NEW EXPRESSIONS

09.05 Look at the words and expressions that are used in the following conversation. Note their meanings.

Que sorte!	*What luck! / How lucky!*
Faz um tempão que não vou para a praia.	*It's ages since I went to the beach.*
Que saudade!	*How I miss it!*
vale a pena	*it's worth it*
gostaria	*I would like*
Não acredito!	*I don't believe it!*
Vai ser o máximo!	*It's going to be brilliant!*
e tal	*and so on / and stuff*
tão legal	*so great*
Mal posso esperar!	*I can hardly wait!*

09.06 *Arnaldo and Beatriz are chatting about their holiday plans.*

1 How long is Arnaldo going to spend at the beach?

Beatriz	Arnaldo, o que você vai fazer durante as férias?
Arnaldo	Eu vou passar oito dias no litoral com meus primos.
Beatriz	Que sorte! Faz um tempão que não vou para a praia. Ai, que saudade!
Arnaldo	Então, vem comigo, Beatriz! Sempre vale a pena – praia, sol, cerveja …
Beatriz	Ah, Arnaldo, você sabe que eu gostaria muito de ir com você, mas não posso.
Arnaldo	Cê vai pra onde?
Beatriz	Vou viajar com a Cecília – vamos para Nova Iorque.
Arnaldo	Não acredito! Vai ser o máximo! Eu também gostaria de ir lá contigo, fazer compras e tal.
Beatriz	Vai ser tão legal, mal posso esperar!

2 Read the conversation again and answer the following questions:

a How does Arnaldo try to tempt Beatriz to go to the beach with him?

b What is Beatriz going to be doing?

c How is Beatriz feeling about the trip?

LANGUAGE TIP

Use any of the following when making arrangements to meet:

tem jeito para quarta-feira	*Wednesday will work / Wednesday is do-able*
não tem jeito para quarta-feira	*Wednesday won't work / Wednesday isn't do-able*
vai dar certo	*that will work*
não vai dar certo	*that isn't going to work*
acho que dá para sexta-feira	*I think Friday will work / I think Friday is do-able*
acho que não dá para sexta-feira	*I don't think Friday will work / I don't think Friday is do-able*

These are all colloquial expressions; you could instead use the less informal **é / não é possível** *that is / isn't possible*.

LANGUAGE TIP

Colloquial expressions:

cê = você	
pro / pra = para o / para a	
super-…	*really…*
beleza!	*fantastic!*
saudade	*nostalgia / homesickness / missing a person or place*

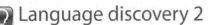

Language discovery 2

1. **How does Beatriz express how long it is since she went to the beach?**
2. **How do you say to someone** *come with me***?**
3. **Which is the verb form meaning** *I would like …***?**
4. **If tão legal means** *so great*, **what might tão bom mean? How would you say** *so cheap***?**

1 FAZ … QUE NÃO … *IT'S … SINCE I …*

Faz + time reference + **que não** + present tense = *it's … since I / we / he, etc. did …*:

Faz cinco horas que ela não come.	*It's five hours since she ate.*
Faz um mês que nós não vamos ao cinema.	*It's a month since we went to the cinema.*
Faz dez anos que eu não vejo meu primo.	*It's ten years since I saw my cousin.*

2 COMMANDS AS INVITATIONS: *COME / GO WITH ME*

Remember that many Brazilians use the more casual forms of verb commands, but you may hear both formal and informal versions. Listen out for the following:

Formal version	Informal version	
venha	**vem**	*come*
vá	**vai**	*go*
olhe	**olha**	*look*
escute	**escuta**	*listen*
ouça	**ouve**	*hear / listen*
tome	**toma**	*take*
diga	**diz**	*say / tell*
pergunte	**pergunta**	*ask*
responda	**responde**	*answer*

3 EXPRESSING *WOULD LIKE (TO) …*

gostaria …	*I / he / she / you* (sing.) *would like (to) …*
gostaríamos …	*we would like (to) …*
gostariam …	*they / you* (pl.) *would like (to) …*

Don't forget to follow the verb with **de** before another verb:

Eu gostaria de viajar.	*I would like to travel.*
O que você gostaria de fazer esta noite?	*What would you like to do tonight?*
Não gostaríamos de visitar. a selva	*We wouldn't like to visit the jungle.*

4 TÃO / TANTO *SO / SO MUCH*

Tão is used before adjectives:

Este vinho é tão caro.	*This wine is so expensive.*
As senhoras são tão simpáticas.	*The ladies are so kind.*

Use **tanto (a / os / as)** with nouns:

Ele tem tanto dinheiro.	*He has so much money.*
Há tantas pessoas que não consigo ver nada.	*There are so many people that I can't see anything.*

Tanto is also used after verbs:

Ela quer ir tanto com ele.	*She wants so much to go with him.*

Practice 2

1 09.07 **Listen to Fátima saying how long it is since she did various things, and decide if the statements are True or False.**

  a It's three years since she visited Salvador.
  b It's ages since she spoke with her cousin.
  c It's two weeks since she went to the club.
  d It's a month since she went to the beach.

2 Translate into English.

  a Artur, vem conosco!
  b Tome o seu troco (*change*)!
  c Venha conhecer o novo shopping!
  d Carla, escuta minha mensagem e me responde!

3 Match the questions and answers.

  a Você gostaria de ir pescar?   **1** Gostariam de relaxar.
  b Vocês gostariam de sair amanhã?   **2** Ela gostaria de ir dançar.

c O que Cíntia gostaria de fazer?

d Como eles gostariam de passar o feriado?

3 Não gostaria, porque não gosto de peixe.

4 Sim, gostaríamos de ir jantar.

4 Complete the sentences with tão or the correct form of tanto.

a Minha irmã é _____ alta (*tall*).

b Elas falam _____ sem parar! Que faladoras (*chatterboxes*)!

c Tem _____ bolos que não sei qual escolher (*to choose*).

d Hoje está _____ frio que não vamos para a praia.

Reading

Look at Amanda's diary for the next week of her holidays and answer the following questions in Portuguese.

segunda-feira	Festa junina no Parque da Cidade às 7 da noite
terça-feira	Campeonato de vôlei de praia (o dia todo)
quarta-feira	visitar o tio Valdir no hospital
quinta-feira	jantar com meus pais
sexta-feira	festa de aniversário do Carlos
sábado	praia de manhã e casamento da Ana à noite

1 Onde a Amanda vai na segunda-feira de noite?

2 Quem ela vai encontrar na quinta-feira?

3 Quando é a festa de aniversário do Carlos?

4 Quando ela vai à praia?

5 O que ela vai fazer na terça-feira?

Listen and understand

 09.08 Listen to a telephone message left on Ricardo's answering machine by a friend and answer the following questions.

1 What is he being invited to?

2 Who can he take with him?

3 When is this event going to be?

Writing

Now reply to Jorge's invitation by email, as though you were Ricardo. Follow the cues and create your response.

1 **Greet Jorge.**
2 **Thank him for the invitation.**
3 **Say** *It would be great but it's not possible; we're going to spend Sunday on the beach*.
4 **Say** *Happy birthday* **(Parabéns!).**
5 **Sign off.**

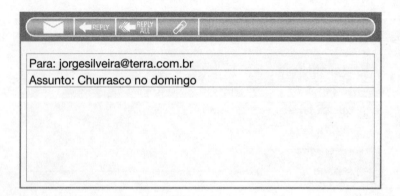

Para: jorgesilveira@terra.com.br
Assunto: Churrasco no domingo

 09.09 Pronunciation practice

The letter **g** has different sounds according to what vowel follows it. Listen now to some examples from the dialogues, plus some additional words, giving you a better idea of pronunciation rules.

Go further

 9.10 The birthday song in Portuguese sounds exactly like in English, but the words are a bit different. Can you guess what each line means?

Parabéns pra você
Nesta data querida
Muitas felicidades
Muitos anos de vida!

Test yourself

1 Identify the odd one out in each of the following.
   a Natal – Reveillon – Páscoa – sábado
   b visitar família – viajar – trabalhar – ir ao clube
   c não tem jeito – dá certo – não posso – não dá
   d irmão – montão – tempão – portão

2 Match the colloquial expressions.
   a super-bonito   **1** How I miss that!
   b Beleza!   **2** really good-looking
   c Que saudade!   **3** Is that so?
   d Que legal!   **4** How brilliant!
   e Ah é?   **5** Fantastic!

3 Try saying the following sentences out loud in Portuguese.
   a Do you have plans for the bank holiday?
   b I'm going to spend the weekend on the coast.
   c Thanks for the invitation!
   d I'd like to visit Brasília.
   e I can hardly wait!

SELF CHECK	
I CAN ...	
⬤	. . . talk about future plans.
⬤	. . . say what I would like to do.
⬤	. . . accept or decline invitations.
⬤	. . . recognize typical Brazilian celebrations.
⬤	. . . discuss typical holiday activities.

10 Você viu o jogo?

Did you see the game?

In this unit, you will learn how to:
▶ *talk about past events.*
▶ *discuss sports and leisure activities.*
▶ *ask and answer questions in the past.*
▶ *describe how good or bad something was.*
▶ *recognize time references in the past.*

CEFR: (A2) *Can ask and answer questions about pastimes; Can describe past activities and personal experiences; Can explain what he/she likes or dislikes about something.*

Lazer

The warm climate makes it possible to spend a lot of leisure time outdoors – **na praia**, **no parque**, **no jardim**, near **cachoeiras** (*waterfalls*) or along **lagos** (*lakes*) or **rios** (*rivers*). Brazilians of all ages love **parques de diversão** (*amusement parks*), and these can get extremely busy in the **alta temporada** (*high season*)! **Futebol** is played on any surface (sand, cement, grass). Volleyball (indoor and outdoor) is also very popular. Many Brazilians have never seen **geada** (*frost*) or **neve** (*snow*), so there are few opportunities for cold-weather activities outdoors – in fact, many people cancel their day out if it starts to rain! Many spend a lot of time on their computers and mobile phones, on social media, checking the news and the weather, and so on. In social gatherings, Brazilians like to talk about **a política** (*politics*), particularly at local level, and **a economia** (*the economy*). Discussions can become very heated and animated, with everybody speaking loudly and at the same time. Restaurants and bars can be very noisy places, as can the family dinner table! Of course, **o jogo** (*the game / match*) is another well-contested debate, whichever team you support.

If you want to save money, when is the best time to go to this amusement park?

> Parque Beto Carrero World
> Entrada Adultos: 1 dia R$80 2 dias R$130
> Crianças de 4 a 9 anos: 1 dia R$60 2 dias R$100
> Crianças a partir de 10 anos pagam como adultos.
> Os preços acima são válidos apenas na baixa temporada!

Vocabulary builder

10.01 Look at the words and phrases and complete the missing English expressions. Then listen and try to imitate the pronunciation of the speakers.

ESPORTES E LAZER	*SPORTS AND LEISURE*
jogar vôlei / basquete	*to play volleyball / basketball*
fazer caminhadas no calçadão	*to stroll along the promenade*
correr na praia	*to run on the beach*
relaxar	_____
ir à academia	*to go to the gym*
encontrar / sair com amigos	*to meet / go out with friends*
ir a uma boate / um show de música	*to go to a club / a music show*
dançar	_____
ir ao cinema / teatro	*to go to the cinema /* _____
ir ao shopping	*to go to the shopping centre*
ver Fórmula 1	*to watch* (lit. *to see*) *Formula 1*
assistir TV / uma novela	*to watch TV / a soap opera*

QUESTIONS IN THE PAST TENSE

O que você fez / viu / comeu?	*What did you do / see / eat?*
Onde você foi / visitou?	*Where did you go /* _____ ?
O que você achou?	*What did you think?*
Você gostou?	*Did you enjoy / like it?*
O que aconteceu?	*What happened?*
Como foi?	*What was it like / How was it?*

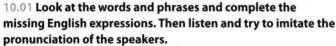

NEW EXPRESSIONS

 10.02 Look at the words and expressions that are used in the following conversation. Note their meanings.

Você viu o jogo ontem à noite?	*Did you see the match last night?*
Não pude assistir.	*I couldn't watch (it).*
Que pena!	*What a shame!*
eles começaram mal	*they started badly*
E daí?	*And then what?*
Daí, virou uma porcaria!	*And then it turned into a shambles!*
o capitão brigou com o árbitro	*the captain argued with the referee*
o Santos ganhou	*Santos won*
Deus me livre de futebol!	*God forbid, football! (lit. God free me from football!)*
Eu fui ao cinema.	*I went to the cinema.*

Conversation 1

 10.03 *Gabriel and Iolanda are in the bar chatting about last night's football.*

1 How does Gabriel describe the match?

Gabriel	Iolanda, você viu o jogo ontem à noite?
Iolanda	Não vi, não. Eu estava trabalhando até tarde e não pude assistir.
Gabriel	Que pena! Foi ótimo!
Iolanda	O que aconteceu, então?
Gabriel	O Botafogo estava ganhando, mas na segunda parte eles começaram mal.
Iolanda	E daí?
Gabriel	Daí, virou uma porcaria! O capitão brigou com o árbitro e recebeu o cartão vermelho.
Iolanda	Incrível! E depois?
Gabriel	Bom, no fim, o Santos ganhou e todo o mundo gostou. Maravilha!
(Another friend, Mário, approaches.)	
Iolanda	Mário, tudo bem? Estávamos falando do jogo. Você viu?
Mário	Eu, não! Deus me livre de futebol! Detesto! Eu fui ao cinema; o filme foi interessantíssimo.

2 Read the conversation again and match the questions and answers.

a Você viu o jogo?
b O que aconteceu?
c E daí?
d E depois?

1 O Botafogo estava ganhando.
2 No fim, o Santos ganhou.
3 Não vi, não.
4 Daí, virou uma porcaria.

HOW TO EXPRESS PAST SEQUENCES	
primeiro	*first*
depois	*then, after*
daí	*and then*
assim	*then, therefore*
então	*and so*
no fim	*in the end*

gosto (muito) / não gosto (nada)	*I like (a lot) / I don't like (at all)*
adoro / detesto	*I love / hate*
não me interessa	*it doesn't interest me*

Language discovery 1

1 Find the Portuguese for the following expressions in the dialogue: *everybody enjoyed / had a good time*; *he received the red card*; *they started badly*.

2 Work out the meaning of the following verbs, all in the first person singular (/): não vi; não pude; eu fui.

3 Which adjectives describe the football match and the film? Which verb is used with both, meaning *it was?*

1 EXPRESSING THE SIMPLE PAST: *I WENT, I ATE, I ENJOYED*

To express what you did, or what you have done, at a specific point in the past, remove the **-ar**, **-er**, **-ir** ending from the infinitive form of a regular verb and follow the pattern for past tense endings as follows:

	-ar → gostar	-er → beber	-ir → abrir
eu	+ei → gostei	+i → bebi	+i → abri
você / ele / ela	+ou → gostou	+eu → bebeu	+iu → abriu
nós	+amos → gostamos	+emos → bebemos	+imos → abrimos
vocês / eles / elas	+aram → gostaram	+eram → beberam	+iram → abriram

Look for patterns to help you remember, e.g. **amos / emos / imos**. These are also the endings used for the *we* verb form in the present tense – you need to look out for past time references to help you distinguish between the two timeframes. This past tense is often called the preterite.

2 IRREGULAR VERBS IN THE PRETERITE: VER / PODER / IR

ver: vi, viu, vimos, viram

poder: pude, pôde, pudemos, puderam

ir: fui, foi, fomos, foram

You will use the preterite of **ir** a lot to express where you went in the past.

3 DESCRIBING HOW SOMETHING WAS: FOI + ADJECTIVE

The Portuguese verb **ser** has the same form in the preterite as **ir**: **fui, foi, fomos, foram**. In practice, it is used extensively in the **foi** form to express *it was* when describing what something was like: **foi ótimo / maravilhoso / interessante / péssimo / ruim** (*awful*) **/ horrível / divertido** (*funny*), etc. Don't forget to change the ending of the adjective if you are describing something feminine.

 Practice 1

1 Form the verbs correctly in the past tense.

   a Eu (relaxar) _____ no clube.

   b Paula (perder = *to lose*) _____ a carteira (*purse / wallet*).

   c As amigas (assistir) _____ a novela.

   d Nós não (visitar) _____ o castelo (*castle*).

   e O ladrão (*thief*) (desaparecer = *to disappear*) _____.

2 Choose the correct response.

   a Vocês viram o futebol ontem?

      1 Sim, vimos.   **2** Sim, vi.

   b Ana jogou tênis com você?

      1 Não, ela não pude.   **2** Não, ela não pôde.

   c Onde você foi no sábado?

      1 Foi à academia.   **2** Fui à academia.

3 10.04 Listen and indicate how each event is described.

   a The film was great / terrible.

   b The show was marvellous / boring.

   c The game was awful / incredible.

   d The soap opera was interesting / funny.

Conversation 2

NEW EXPRESSIONS

10.05 Look at the words and expressions that are used in the following conversation. Note their meanings.

Decidi ir ao shopping.	*I decided to go to the shopping centre.*
Só paguei dez reais cada.	*I only paid ten reais each.*
Uma pechincha!	*A bargain!*
já que …	*(seeing) as … / given that*
Me diverti muito.	*I really enjoyed myself.*
Tlve que voltar antes do fim.	*I had to go home* (lit. *return*) *before the end.*
Não fiz nada.	*I didn't do anything.*
Fiquei em casa.	*I stayed at home.*
Ela disse que …	*She said that …*

10.06 *Priscila and Vicente are chatting on the phone about what they did at the weekend.*

1 What did Priscila buy?

Vicente	Oi, Priscila, tudo bem? Me conta, o que você fez no fim de semana?
Priscila	No sábado meus pais estavam visitando família, então decidi ir ao shopping.
Vicente	O que você comprou?
Priscila	Hah! – comprei uma bolsa e duas saias; só paguei dez reais cada. Uma pechincha! E você?
Vicente	Bom, já que gosto tanto de música clássica, fui a um show na praça.
Priscila	Legal! Você gostou?
Vicente	Me diverti muito, mas tive que voltar antes do fim para pegar o ônibus. Foi uma pena!
Priscila	Eu, no domingo, não fiz nada. Fiquei em casa dormindo.
Vicente	Preguiçosa! Eu me encontrei com sua prima e fomos àquele novo bar.
Priscila	Ah é? O que ela falou de mim?
Vicente	Hmm – ela disse que você é … *(telephone connection is lost).*

2 Read, then listen to, the whole conversation again and answer the questions.

  a What were Priscila's parents doing on Saturday?

  b Where did Vicente go?

  c Why did he have to leave early?

  d Who did Vicente meet on Sunday?

> **LANGUAGE TIP**
>
> Remember! Casual language: **me diverti / me encontrei / me conta**; formal language: **diverti-me / encontrei-me / conte-me**

 Language discovery 2

  a **Find the expressions in the dialogue that mean:** *I didn't do anything / I had to return / She said.*

  b **Which -ar verbs do paguei and fiquei come from?**

  c **Find three past time references; which preposition, denoting** *in / on / at,* **do they have in common?**

1 MORE IRREGULAR PRETERITES: FAZER (*TO DO, MAKE*) **/ TER** (*TO HAVE*) **/ DIZER** (*TO SAY, TELL*)

Fazer: fiz / fez / fizemos / fizeram

Ter: tive / teve / tivemos / tiveram

Dizer: disse / disse / dissemos / disseram

2 SPELLING CHANGES IN THE PRETERITE: VERBS ENDING IN -CAR AND -GAR

In the first person (*I*) in the preterite, compare what happens with a regular **-ar** verb and those ending in **-car** and **-gar**:

comprar ⟶ comprei

ficar ⟶ fiquei

pagar ⟶ paguei

-car and **-gar** verbs do this to maintain a hard **c** or **g** sound. Without the change, the letters **c** and **g** when followed by **e** make soft sounds, and would therefore deviate from the sound of the original verb. More typical examples include: **brincar** *to play*, **explicar** *to explain*, **tocar** *to touch / to play an instrument*, **chegar** *to arrive*, **jogar** *to play sport / games*, **entregar** *to hand over*.

3 EXPRESSING THE PAST: *LAST WEEK*, *ON MONDAY*, **ETC.**

Use time references you already know along with a verb in the preterite to denote an event that has happened, e.g.,

no sábado fomos ao clube   *on Saturday we went to the club*

na quarta-feira trabalhei   *on Wednesday I worked*

Other useful time expressions include: **no domingo passado, a semana passada**, **o ano passado**, etc.; **ontem** (*yesterday*); **ontem à noite**, **ontem de manhã**, **ontem de tarde**. Don't forget you can also use references to clock time, such as **às dez e vinte ela pegou o ônibus**.

 Practice 2

1 Choose the correct verb form.

   a Eu fiz / fez um bolo de aniversário.

   b Vocês tiveram / tivemos muita sorte.

   c O que ela disseram / disse?

   d Nós não fez / fizemos barulho (*noise*).

   e Marcos teve / tive que ir trabalhar.

2 Form the verbs correctly in the preterite.

   a jogar ⟶ Eu _____ vôlei na praia.

   b explicar ⟶ A professor _____ a lição.

   c brincar ⟶ Eu não _____ ontem.

   d pagar ⟶ Você _____ a conta?

   e chegar ⟶ Eu _____ às 11 horas.

3 Translate into Portuguese.

   a Last week I played basketball.

   b Yesterday we went to the theatre.

   c The film ended at 9.30 p.m.

   d On Thursday she went to the gym.

Reading and writing

1 **You go to the beach and see this sign. Can you get the gist of it and say whether each statement is True or False? You may have to do this for real on a beach in Brazil!**

> **PERIGO: AVISO DE RESSACA NO MAR**
>
> Cuidado. Mantenha-se à distância.
>
> Mar agitado, ventos fortes e ondas violentas de mais de três metros

a This is an advert for a surfing competition.
b It is dangerous to swim in the sea today.
c It is a good day for sailing.
d You are advised to stay away from the sea today.

2 **Ana is on holiday in Florianópolis with her family. After a fun day at Beto Carrero World, one of the largest amusement parks in Brazil, she sends an email to her friends in Brasília. Fill in the gaps in the text with the correct word.**

dentro   dormir   no   cara   tanto

| ✉ | ⬅ REPLY | ⬅⬅ REPLY ALL | 📎 |

Oi gente! A entrada _____ parque foi _____, mas valeu a pena! Adorei a montanha russa, o barco Viking e os shows ao vivo. Gritamos muito _____ do trem fantasma!!! Adorei! Me diverti _____ que estou pregada! Agora vou _____. Beijinhos, Ana

montanha russa	rollercoaster
fantasma	ghost
pregada(o)	(slang) exhausted, very tired

3 10.07 **Pronunciation practice**

In Brazilian Portuguese, an **-i** at the end of a word has a different sound from its English equivalent – it's almost as if there were a **w** before it. Listen to some examples now and repeat after the native speaker.

Now listen and practise how these common combined vowels sound:

-oi

-ai

-ei

Listen and understand

10.08 **Three people report various incidents to the police. Listen to each one and write down in English what happened in each case.**

	What happened?	When?
João		
Carolina		
Jair		

Go further

Paulo and Vilma have just moved home and have sent the following message to all their friends:

> Queridos amigos,
>
> Resolvemos mudar para o litoral. Já vendemos nossa casa no interior e compramos um apartamento de dois quartos com varanda no litoral. Agora podemos ir à praia a pé! Que maravilha! Realizamos um sonho antigo!
>
> Abraços a todos,
> Paulo e Vilma

Now fill in the gaps with the verbs from the text above in the 3rd person plural (eles), in the past tense:

Paulo e Vilma _____ mudar para o litoral. Eles já _____ a sua casa no interior e _____ um apartamento no litoral. Agora eles podem ir à praia a pé. Eles _____ um sonho antigo.

 ## Test yourself

1 10.09 Listen to Fernanda describe her weekend and put the activities in the correct order.

a ir ao cinema
b passar a manhã no clube
c encontrar Ana
d assistir um show
e ficar em casa
f ir fazer compras
g ver TV

2 Fill the gaps in this dialogue with expressions from the box.

voltei   ontem   ótimo
Adorei!   uma boate

Antônio   Você saiu _____ à noite?
Jorge   Saí, sim. Fui a _____ com meus colegas.
Antônio   Vocês se divertiram?
Jorge   Muitíssimo! Dançamos muito e só _____ para casa às três horas da manhã.
Antônio   Você gostou então?
Jorge   _____ Foi _____

3 Have a go at answering these in Portuguese any way you wish.
   a O que você fez ontem?
   b Onde você foi no sábado?
   c Você gostou da música?
   d Como foi o jogo?
   e Onde você visitou?

SELF CHECK

	I CAN ...
◐	. . . talk about past events.
◐	. . . discuss sports and leisure activities.
◐	. . . ask and answer questions in the past.
◐	. . . describe how good or bad something was.
◯	. . . recognize time references in the past.

1 **Make full sentences by matching the first part in the left-hand column with the second part from the right-hand column.**

a	Estou pensando em visitar	**1**	na escola.
b	João está trabalhando	**2**	pelo interior.
c	Nós estávamos viajando	**3**	chopes.
d	Isabel estava pensando em comprar	**4**	os meus avós.
e	Eles estão bebendo	**5**	uma nova saia.

2 **10.10 Using the cues, follow the dialogue on the audio and speak your part during the pauses on the audio. You will hear the correct version after each pause.**

a Start by saying *Good afternoon!*

b Say *I have a reservation: a single room reserved for three nights.*

c Give your own name in full.

d Spell your own surname.

e Say *Here.*

f Ask *At what time is breakfast served?*

g Say *Thank you.*

3 **10.11 Listen, and indicate in English what each problem is.**

a _____

b _____

c _____

d _____

e _____

4 **Choose the odd one out in each sequence.**

a	no canto	no fim	ao lado	ao meio-dia
b	hóspede	cama	cofre	despertador
c	calça	terno	preço	vestido
d	amarelo	tamanho	roxo	cinza
e	pescar	jogar	correr	comer

5 10.12 **Listen to people talking about things they have done in the past, and complete the missing information in Portuguese. Use the third person singular or plural (*he / she, they*) of each verb.**

	Quando?	O quê?	Com quem?
a	no fim de semana		
b		teve o batizado da sobrinha	
c			os primos
d	no feriado		
e			as amigas foram / ela não

6 10.13 **Try saying these words out loud, then listen to the correct version on the audio.**

> Nova Iorque caixa gente
> oi! ritmo bege legal
> maio táxi segundo
> Brasil falei

7 **You are looking for clothing in a fashion store. Complete your side of the dialogue.**

Empregada	Pois não?
You	Say *Good morning. I'm looking for a green shirt; what do you have in a large?*
Empregada	Bom, temos estas, de algodão – muito elegantes.
You	Say *How much is it?*
Empregada	47 reais cada. São as mais baratas que temos.
You	Say *I don't really like the colour. Do you have any in blue?*
Empregada	Em azul? Deixe ver – temos aquelas ali de manga curta em várias cores.
You	Say *May I try on that one you have there?*
Empregada	À vontade. O provador é no canto, à direita.
(Five minutes later)	
You	Say *It's very large. Don't you have a smaller one?*
Empreg.	Em azul não temos, infelizmente. Na próxima semana …
You	Say *What a shame! Thanks.*

8 10.14 **Listen to a radio advertisement and answer True or False for each question.**

a It's an ad for a new supermarket.   T/F
b It's summertime.   T/F
c The event is on 16 June.   T/F
d The event takes place in Republic Square.   T/F
e Listeners are asked to name the most popular   T/F
    film of the summer.
f One of the prizes is a trip to Rio.   T/F

9 **Look at the brochure and then complete each sentence with an appropriate word.**

Hotel Fazenda das Amoreiras – a natureza nas suas mãos!

apartamentos de luxo

piscina tropical

quadra de tênis

sala de fitness

5 km de trilhas

lagos

– cachoeiras

churrasqueira

bar e música

restaurante

Abertura do restaurante:

Café da manhã: 06:30 – 07:30 – café, sucos e pãezinhos

07:30 – 10:30 – café da manhã buffet

Almoço: 12:30 – 15:00 – almoços e refeições ligeiras

Jantar: A partir das 19:00

O 'bar Flor da Selva' fica aberto das 11:30 até às 02:00 para refeições ligeiras, pizzas, chá e bolos, e uma variedade de bebidas nacionais e internacionais.

No Hotel Fazenda das Amoreiras há várias atividades de lazer nas quais você poderia participar: Pode nadar na _____; pode _____ tênis; pode _____ trilha. Também, você poderia _____ no lago, _____ churrasco, ou dançar no _____.

10 Now answer the following questions.

a What type of accommodation is offered?
b What natural features are advertised?
c What is offered for breakfast for early risers?
d Where can you eat between 3 p.m. and 7 p.m.?
e What is on offer at the 'Flor da Selva' bar as well as pizzas?

Answer key

Brazil
south region, north region, centre-west region

Vocabulary builder
Greetings Good, How, See you

Conversation 1
1 Ana **2a** morning **b** lawyer **c** José dos Santos **3a** True **b** False **c** False

Language discovery 1
1a Eu **b** Ele **2a** estou **b** sou **3a** está means 'you are/are you' **b** Estou means ' I am'

Practice 1
1a você **b** ele **c** eu **d** nós **2a** médica **b** teacher **c** gerente **d** enfermeira **e** eletricista **3a** está **b** Sou **c** Estou **d** é **4a** 3 **b** 4 **c** 1 **d** 2 **5a** Ana – argentina, advogada **b** Peter – alemão, engenheiro **c** Isabel – portuguesa, cozinheira **d** Paulo – brasileiro, médico **6a** nome **b** de / trabalho **c** Sou / própria **d** chamo-me **e** é **7a** Carlos is in a hurry. **b** Joaquim is hungry. **c** Anita is cold. **d** Catarina is hot.

Conversation 2
1 English and Spanish **2a** Italian **b** Toulouse **c** English and German **d** No **e** Ornella's **f** Argentina

Language discovery 2
1a Você fala inglês? **b** falo inglês **2** I am English … I speak French.

Practice 2
1a -o **b** -am **c** -a **d** -amos **2a** Você não é de Londres. **b** Meu nome não é Marcus. **c** Paulo não fala alemão. **d** Ela não é americana. **3a** italiana **b** alemão **c** francês **d** espanhola **4a** Falo um pouco de português. **b** Não falo grego. **c** Falamos francês bem.

Reading
a False **b** False **c** True **d** False

Reading and writing
a agora / em **b** de / mas **c** Sou / moro **d** Sou de Brasília, mas agora moro em Londres **e** (sample answer) Sou de Sydney, mas agora moro em Washington.

Speaking
(sample answers) **1a** Sim, sou americana. **b** Não, não falo inglês. **c** Sim, o Roberto é de São Paulo. **d** Eu moro em Manchester. **e** Não, a Cristina não é minha amiga.

Test yourself
1a 4 **b** 1 **c** 5 **d** 2 **e** 3 **2a** dia / Como **b** Este **c** tudo **d** Muito **3a** Nós falamos inglês. **b** Elas não falam português. **c** Vocês falam grego?

UNIT 2
Os brasileiros
João is saying: I'm single, I'm a civil servant and I don't speak English.

Vocabulary builder
Family girlfriend, daughter, sister

Conversation 1
1 Luciana **2a** yes, one son **b** Felipe, Fernando's son **c** Rosa's husband

Language discovery 1
1 tenho **2** vende **3** um, uma – masculine and feminine

Practice 1
1a tem **b** tenho **c** temos **d** tem **2a** vende **b** como **c** bebem **d** escrevemos **e** corre **3a** um filho **b** uma namorada **c** o advogado **d** a mãe **4a** seis, sete **b** vinte e sete **c** noventa e dois **d** sessenta, oitenta **e** trinta, trinta e cinco **5a** Fábio is 21. **b** He studies civil engineering. **c** Heloísa is 19. **d** Their mother is a nurse.

Conversation 2
1 22 years old **2a** True **b** True **c** False **d** False **e** True

Language discovery 2
1 bonita **2** mais velho, mais nova **3** his birthday's in April **4** singular and plural

Practice 2
1a 2 **b** 4 **c** 1 **d** 3 **2a** 3 **b** 2 **c** 1 **d** 4 **3a** Faço anos em março. **b** Ele faz anos em dezembro. **c** Quando você faz anos? **d** Elas fazem anos em agosto. **4a** as minhas irmãs **b** os seus empregados **c** as nossas casas **d** os meus tios

Reading and writing
1 é / em / de / Tenho / sou / minha / dois **2a** She is 25. **b** She was born in Taubaté. **c** She is single. **d** She lives in São Paulo, with her parents and her two brothers.

Listen and understand
1 c **2** e **3** b

Test yourself
1a marido **b** pais **c** solteiros **d** mãe **2** Marcos **3** 12 16 22 38 85 74 **4a** Você é casada? **b** Quantos anos você tem? **c** Você tem filhos? **d** Que lindo / Que bonito! / Que gato! **e** Onde ele estuda?

UNIT 3
A cozinha brasileira
It means: Joana's black bean stew is excellent. She's a good cook.

Vocabulary builder
Drinks/Food mineral, wine, milk, sandwich, chocolate

Conversation 1
1 draught beer **2a** passion fruit, banana and lemon juice **b** fried cassava **c** afternoon / early evening **3 Jorge:** Boa tarde. Um bauru, um x-búrguer e uma porção de mandioca frita. **Mariana:** Um suco de maracujá, banana e limão, e um chope. Obrigada.

Language discovery 1
1 quer / quero / posso? **2** very **3** gosto

Practice 1
1a posso **b** quer **c** deveria **d** devem **2a** realmente **b** bastante **c** um pouco
d muito **3a** bons **b** má **c** bom **d** maus **4a** likes chocolate **b** hates wine **c**
can't stand eggs

Conversation 2
1 tomato salad **2a** rice, chips and beetroot salad **b** red house wine **c** pavê

Language discovery 2
1 masculine / feminine **2** divido com você **3** grelhado / fritas

Practice 2
1a da **b** dos **c** de **d** das **e** do **2a** Divido com você. **b** O banco abre amanhã.
c Nós não partimos hoje. **d** Roberta decide beber água. **3a** 3 **b** 4 **c** 1 **d** 2

Listen and understand
Márcia wants a salad and a salmon sandwich. **Guilherme** wants rump
steak, rice, beans and chips.

Reading and writing
1 adoro / comida / favorito / peixe / adoramos **2 a** True **b** True **c** False

Test yourself
1 The missing menu items are: cenoura / peixe / assado / branco / doce
2 Silvana orders starter: beetroot salad, main and accompaniment: grilled
fish with rice and chips, dessert: lemon mousse, drink: espresso **3 You:**
Bom dia. Um sanduíche de presunto e uma porção de mandioca frita. /
Um suco de laranja com acerola por favor.

REVIEW 1
1 a sou **b** têm **c** está **d** somos **e** tem **f** estão **2a** Onde você trabalha?
b O Fernando come peixe? **c** Quando vocês partem? **d** Você gosta de
cerveja? **e** Eles vendem queijo? **3a** Ele é alto. **b** As minhas irmãs não
são gordas. **c** Ela tem olhos verdes. **d** A sopa está fria. **e** Os sucos são
deliciosos. **f** Ela é muito bonita/linda. **4a** marido / 57 / seis / março **b**
filha / 19 / quinze / junho **c** tia / 72 / vinte e um / setembro **d** primo / 6
/ trinta / novembro **e** avó / 91 / dois / maio. The youngest is the cousin.
The oldest is the grandmother. The aunt's birthday is in September. **6**
You: no starter/main – porco grelhado / dessert – pavê de abacaxi /
drink – caipirinha. **Samuel:** starter – salada de palmito / main – galinha

assada / dessert – salada de frutas / drink – cerveja. **Patrícia:** starter – salada de palmito / main – ovos recheados / dessert – sorvete / drink – suco. **7** (sample answers): **a** Vou bem. **b** Eu me chamo/chamo-me Bob. **c** Trabalho num supermercado. **d** Sim, falo francês bem. **e** Moro em Liverpool. **f** O meu email é … **g** O número do meu celular é 000777444. **h** Sou de Berlim. **i** Não, sou divorciado. **j** Sim, tenho dois filhos. **k** Tenho 35 anos. **l** Faço anos em agosto. **8 Maria:** Lisbon / Portuguese / doctor / married / 0753-00218. **Bruno:** Brazilian (but he and family from Italy) / Brasília / student / Portuguese, Italian, Spanish / 0371-4825555. **9** Boa noite! Para começar, uma salada de cenoura. / O que recomenda? / Prefiro peixe. / Está bem OR tudo bem. / Uma garrafa do vinho da casa./ Branco. E uma garrafa de água mineral com gás por favor. / Um mousse de chocolate, por favor. / Sim, obrigada OR por favor, e a conta.

UNIT 4
Rotinas típicas
In the morning I drink a cup of coffee and eat two pieces of toast with butter before going to work.

Vocabulary builder
Frequency morning, night, rarely **Countries** France, Germany

Conversation 1
1 No, in France he teaches only in the morning **2a** False – he IS enjoying his visit **b** True **c** True

Language discovery 1
1 gostando **2** no – m / f **3** conhecer / sei

Practice 1
1a está comendo **b** estão gostando **c** estou trabalhando **d** estamos partindo **2a** na **b** nas **c** no **d** em **e** nos **3a** 3 **b** 1 **c** 4 **d** 2

Conversation 2
1 Gabriela yes, Sérgio rarely **2a** 7 hours a day **b** the gym **c** Wednesdays **d** normally at the weekend

Language discovery 2
1 myself **2** me divirto muito **3** segunda

Practice 2
1a se **b** me **c** nos **d** se **2a** Não, não me sinto triste. **b** Sim, eu sempre me divirto na praia. **c** Não, nunca me sirvo no restaurante. **d** Não, eu me visto de manhã. **3a** 3ª visitar amigos. **b** 5ª trabalhar. **c** sáb. Fazer compras.

Reading and writing
1a Ele está lendo o jornal. **b** Ele está jogando futebol. **c** Ela está vendo televisão. **d** Ele está nadando. **2** viajando / gostando / passando / comprando **3a** estou passando **b** estamos visitando **c** estamos gastando **d** está comendo **e** estão vendo

Listen and understand
a She gets up early, makes breakfast and takes the kids to school. **b** On Wednesdays. **c** On Monday and Wednesday. **d** On Tuesday and Thursday. **e** At home.

Go further
Eduardo Guedes is a famous chef in Brazil. He is from São Paulo. He presents a food programme on a TV channel from Monday to Friday. Sometimes he leaves the studio and travels to various parts of Brazil, preparing delicious dishes from different states and regions. We can see the recipes and the videos on the internet.

Test yourself
1a Portugal **b** Espanha **c** China **d** Canadá **e** França **2a** trabalhar / 35 horas por semana. **b** ir na academia / muitas vezes **c** preparar o café da manhã / geralmente não **d** ir à igreja / todos os domingos **3a** Trabalho trinta horas por semana. **b** Nas sextas janto fora. **c** Eu me levanto cedo. **d** Sempre faço exercício nos sábados.

UNIT 5
Transportes no Brasil
'stopping for 25 minutes'

Vocabulary builder
Travel information ticket, student, last

Conversation 1
1 8 hours 45 minutes **2a** 8.30 p.m. **b** Saturday **c** student card

Language discovery 1
1 A que horas **2** vinte e trinta / oito e meia da noite **3** duzentos e setenta e cinco

Practice 1
1a começa / concerto **b** chega / ônibus **c** parte / avião **d** abre / banco
2a às dez para as oito (da manhã) **b** às duas e meia (da tarde) **c** às seis e cinco (da tarde) **d** às quinze para as dez (da noite) **e** à meia-noite **3a** cento e vinte e seis **b** quatrocentos e noventa e um **c** oitocentos e trinta e dois **d** setecentos e setenta e cinco **e** trezentos e noventa
4 The correct order is: 232 970 681 599 242

Conversation 2
1 platform 5 **2a** True **b** True **c** False **d** True **e** False

Language discovery 2
1 para / para / pela **2** Ser (são) **3** vem

Practice 2
1a para **b** por **c** para **d** pelo **e** para **2a** 13:00 **b** 07:55 **c** 14:30 **d** 22:00 **3a** vou **b** vamos **c** vem **d** vêm **e** vão

Reading and writing
1a vai / carro **b** vou / bicicleta **c** vamos / avião **2** Há / Tem ônibus para Belo Horizonte de manhã? / Quanto é / custa o ônibus leito? / Quero / Queria duas passagens para sexta-feira de manhã. **3a** São oito horas. **b** São nove e vinte e cinco **c** São três e meia

Listen and understand
1a at 8:15 a.m. **b** at 11 a.m. **c** at 3 p.m. **d** at 6:30 p.m.

Go further
1a three **b** 1 p.m. **c** behind **d** last Sunday **2a** 3 **b** 3

Test yourself
1a horário **b** plataforma **c** para **d** venho **2a** 3 **b** 1 **c** 4 **d** 2 **3a** 11:10 **b** Copacabana **c** 12

UNIT 6
No centro da cidade
250 is the number of the building in Cabo Frio Avenue. He lives in apartment number 602. Jardim Alvorada is the name of the **bairro** *(district)*. 860620-630 is the postcode. Londrina is the name of the city. PR is the abbreviation of the state name, Paraná.

Vocabulary builder
City centre market, centre, traffic **Directions** front, far (off / away)

Conversation 1
1 Republic Square **2a** she has to turn left here **b** go to the square and ask again **c** can she see that set of traffic lights over there?

Language discovery 1
1 à esquerda **2** pode / poderia – one means 'can you', the other means 'could you' **3** passar / cruzar

Practice 1
1a à **b** aos **c** às **d** ao **2a** você pode me indicar / mostrar no mapa? **b** você pode repetir por favor? **c** você poderia me trazer o cardápio? **d** você pode me ajudar? **3a** pass through the square **b** take the third street on the right **c** carry straight on **d** go up here **4** the correct order is c / a / b

Conversation 2
1 second floor **2a** no, she doesn't know **b** an internet café **c** go and see what films are on at the cinema

Language discovery 2
1 neste **2** vire instead of vira – vire is the direct command 'turn!'; vira means 'you turn' **3** at / to the, of the **4** pertinho

Practice 2
1a nesta **b** nestas **c** naquela **d** naqueles **2a** tome **b** passe **c** vá **d** cruze **3a** small shop / uma loja **b** small bar / um bar **c** some small streets / uma rua **d** a small school / uma escola **4a** livraria Santos **b** correio **c** Central de Informação Turística (CIT)

Listen and understand
1 in front of the Machado shoe shop **2** Cross the street and walk in the direction of the park. **3** Turn left. **4** Number 510 **5** Apartment 204

Writing
horas / ponto / leva / chegar / antes

Go further
a emergency exit **b** underground parking **c** lifts **d** cashier **e** no smoking **f** open **g** closed **h** restaurant on the 3rd floor

Test yourself
1a 3 **b** 1 **c** 4 **d** 5 **e** 2 **2a** farmácia **b** avenida **c** direita **d** segunda **e** banco **3a** 2ª **b** 5° **c** 7° **d** 1ª **e** 10ª

REVIEW 2
1a come **b** bebo **c** conhecemos **d** comem **e** bebe **f** conhece **2a** At 6:30 a.m. **b** a piece of bread with cheese and a small cup of coffee **c** on Saturday, at 10:30 a.m. **d** She goes to church with her family and then they have lunch at a 'quilo' restaurant. **3a** em **b** na / no **c** no / de **d** no / de **e** de / na **4a** Ele está bebendo café. **b** Ela está dormindo. **c** Ele está comendo um sanduíche. **d** Ele está lendo um livro. **6** A que horas há/tem ônibus para Petrópolis? / Quanto custa? / Quanto é? / Quanto tempo leva? / Uma passagem de ida e volta, por favor. **7a** Monday **b** 10 reais **c** It is free. **8a** Sabe onde é / fica o Palácio de Cristal? **b** O Palácio de Cristal é longe? **c** Pode me mostrar no mapa? **9** d **10** b, e, a, f, c, d **11a** 410 **b** 550 **c** 178 **d** 925 **e** 233 **12a** 5 **b** 4 **c** 1 **d** 2 **e** 3 **13a** Quando **b** Como **c** Quanto tempo **d** Onde **e** O que

UNIT 7
Alojamento
hotel-fazenda

Vocabulary builder
in the hotel: family / meal / access; **in the room:** air conditioning

Conversation 1
1 Room booked for eight nights **2a** 3 **b** 2 **c** 1 **d** 4

Language discovery 1

1 Como se escreve o seu sobrenome? **2** Quais são os seus nomes? Every word has become plural. **3** partir – usually means to leave **4** de fácil acesso / deserta / movimentada

Practice 1

1a White **b** Pereira **c** Olivetti **2a** fácil **b** hotéis **c** lençóis **d** espanhol **e** azul **3a** Tem / Há café da manhã a partir das sete horas. **b** Tem / Há música de quinta(-feira) a sábado. **c** Servem almoço do meio-dia até as duas e trinta / meia. **d** A partir de novembro tem / há muitos visitantes. **4a** movimentada **b** pequenos **c** inteligente **d** feias

Conversation 2

1 the meeting room **2** gym open from 6 a.m. to 11 p.m. **3a** left **b** underground / under the hotel **c** it's dirty and needs to be cleaned **d** at any time

Language discovery 2

1 chegar / acabar – to finish **2** there's a booklet missing – falta um livrinho **3** reunião **4** fechada / suja

Practice 2

1a 3 **b** 4 **c** 1 **d** 2 **2a** a towel **b** information **c** sheets **d** milk **e** three plates **3a** aviões / avião **b** estações / estação **c** órgãos / órgão **4a** estou cansada **b** está frio **c** estão abertas **d** estamos tristes

Reading and listening

1 walking and bicycle rides **2** 60 rooms **3** delicious fish dishes **4** sauna / squash / tennis **5** c **6** a **7** c

Reading

a 3 **b** 4 **c** 2 **d** 1

Go further

Typical check-in information:

Nome: Mary	Sobrenome: Jones
Data de nascimento : 23/09/1954	Local de nascimento: Christ church, Nova Zelândia
Número da Identidade/passaporte: 0987BZMJ1178	
Endereço: 23 Market Street, Glasgow, Escócia, GL45 6NH	

Test yourself
1a Queria me informar sobre as praias. **b** Ao fim do corredor tem a sala de reuniões. **c** Quais são as horas de abertura? **d** Pode comer no bar a qualquer hora. **2a** solteiro. **b** três / 3 **c** Martin **d** 56 **3a** Tenho uma reserva. **b** Temos um quarto / um apartamento reservado para cinco noites. **c** A que horas servem o café da manhã? **d** O quarto / O apartamento tem cofre?

UNIT 8
Fazendo compras
The sign means 'sale' – 40% discount on items paid for there and then or by instalments

Vocabulary builder
Clothing / clothes blouse, sandals **Colours** white, green, beige

Conversation 1
1a black blouse **2a** 65 reais each **b** over there on the left **c** Vanda's skirt

Language discovery 1
1 uma blusa preta / uma blusa branca **2** aquelas ali **3** cara / mais barata / as mais bonitas – all are feminine to agree with blusa

Practice 1
1a verde **b** amarelas **c** marrons **d** roxa **2a** este vestido aqui **b** aquelas camisetas ali **c** esse relógio aí **d** estes cintos aqui **3** nova / fresca / mais /o mais

Conversation 2
1 a pair of flip-flops in orange and blue **2** música popular brasileira (Brazilian pop music) **3a** False **b** False **c** True

Language discovery 2
1 lindíssimas / baratíssimos **2** Que tal …? **3** vinte e cinco mil / quarenta e oito mil **4** dá-me / me dê

Practice 2
1a gordíssimo **b** baratíssimas **c** ótima **d** chatíssimo **e** caríssimos **2a** a small towel **b** the bag in green **c** why not buy five? **3a** 2.518 **b** 1975 **c** 36.400 **d** 1.089 **e** 72.462 **4** me telefona / me manda / me conta

Reading
1a 6 **b** 1 **c** 6 **d** 1 **e** 4 **f** 8 **g** 7 **h** 2 **i** 8 **j** 4 **k** 5

Listen and understand
1 short-sleeved **2** large **3** white

Test yourself
1a biquíni **b** relógio **c** sapatos **d** terno **e** vestido **2a** True **b** False
c False **d** True

UNIT 9
Celebrações
Invitation to: a christening, birthday, 15th birthday party, wedding

Vocabulary builder
Holidays: week, Carnival, Independence **Activities:** to visit the family

Conversation 1
1 by spending a few hours at the club **2a** staying in the swimming pool
b her nephew's christening **c** the next weekend

Language discovery 1
1 tô (estou) pensando/estávamos pensando **2** formal: conosco / informal:
com a gente **3** it makes it seem larger **4** fim de semana, amendoim

Practice 1
1a 3 **b** 4 **c** 1 **d** 5 **e** 2 **2a** com eles **b** comigo **c** com a gente **d** contigo
3a gatão **b** um tempão **c** um garrafão **d** cachorrão **e** beijão **f** abração
4 jardins; mensagens; som; bombons; nuvem

Conversation 2
1 8 days **2a** he says it's worth it – beach, sun, beer … **b** going to New York
with Cecília **c** she can't wait

Language discovery 2
1 faz um tempão que não vou para a praia **2** vem comigo **3** gostaria **4** so
good / tão barato

Practice 2

1a True **b** False **c** True **d** True **2a** Arthur, come with us! **b** Take your change! **c** Come and see the new shopping centre! **d** Carla, listen to my message and answer me! **3a** 3 **b** 4 **c** 2 **d** 1 **4a** tão **b** tanto **c** tantos **d** tão

Reading

1 Ela vai à festa junina no Parque da Cidade. **2** Ela vai encontrar os pais dela. **3** A festa de aniversário do Carlos é na sexta-feira. **4** Ela vai à/na praia no sábado de manhã. **5** Ela vai ao campeonato de vôlei de praia.

Listen and understand

1 A barbecue **2** His wife and his daughter. **3** Next Sunday

Writing

(sample answer): Oi Jorge! Obrigado pelo convite para o churrasco. Seria ótimo, mas não vai dar certo – vamos passar o domingo na praia. Parabéns! Tchau! Ricardo.

Go further

Birthday song: happy birthday (congratulations) to you, on this dear date, many joys (much happiness), many years of life!

Test yourself

1a sábado **b** trabalhar **c** dá certo **d** irmão **2a** 2 **b** 5 **c** 1 **d** 4 **e** 3 **3a** Você tem planos para o feriado? **b** Vou passar o fim de semana no litoral. **c** Obrigado/a pelo convite! **d** Gostaria de visitar Brasília. **e** Mal posso esperar!

UNIT 10
Lazer
The best time to visit the amusement park is in low season.

Vocabulary builder
Sports and leisure to relax, to dance, theatre **Past tense** visit

Conversation 1
1a It was great! **2a** 3 **b** 1 **c** 4 **d** 2

Language discovery 1
1 todo o mundo gostou; recebeu o cartão vermelho; eles começaram mal **2** I didn't see / watch; I couldn't; I went **3** ótimo, interessantíssimo; foi

Practice 1
1a relaxei **b** perdeu **c** assistiram **d** visitamos **e** desapareceu **2a** 1 **b** 2 **c** 2
3a great **b** marvellous **c** awful **d** funny

Conversation 2
1 a bag and two skirts **2a** visiting family **b** a show in the square **c** to catch
the bus **d** Priscila's cousin

Language discovery 2
1 Não fiz nada / tive que voltar / ela disse **2** pagar / ficar **3** no fim de
semana / no sábado / no domingo; no (em)

Practice 2
1a fiz **b** tiveram **c** disse **d** fizemos **e** teve **2a** joguei **b** explicou **c** brinquei
d pagou **e** cheguei **3a** A semana passada eu joguei basquete. **b** Ontem
fomos ao teatro. **c** O filme terminou às nove e trinta. **d** Na quinta-feira ela
foi à academia.

Reading and writing
1a False **b** True **c** False **d** True **2** no / cara / dentro / tanto / dormir

Listen and understand
João: His house was robbed. They took the TV, the computer and some
clothes. It happened at the weekend. **Carolina:** She lost her wallet at the
shopping centre this afternoon. It had a credit card and 150 reais in it. **Jair:**
His dog Guga disappeared yesterday morning.

Go further
resolveram / venderam / compraram / realizaram

Test yourself
1 Correct order: ir fazer compras / encontrar Ana / ir ao cinema / ficar
em casa / ver TV / passar a manhã no clube / assistir um show **2** ontem /
uma boate / voltei / Adorei! / ótimo **3** (sample answers): **a** Ontem fui fazer
compras. **b** No sábado fui à praia. **c** Sim, gostei muito. **d** O jogo foi ruim.
e Visitei a Espanha.

REVIEW 3

1a 4 **b** 1 **c** 2 **d** 5 **e** 3 **2** Boa tarde. / Tenho uma reserva; um quarto de solteiro reservado para três noites. / (sample answer) Sandra Brown. / (sample answer) B-R-O-W-N. / Aqui. / A que horas servem o café da manhã? / Obrigado/a. **3a** shower doesn't work **b** there aren't any towels **c** the plate's dirty **d** there's a lot of noise **e** there's no internet access **4a** ao meio-dia **b** hóspede **c** preço **d** tamanho **e** comer **5a** saiu dançar / com o amigo **b** no sábado passado/toda a família **c** em agosto / foi a um concerto de música rock **d** relaxou no clube / o namorado. **e** durante as férias da Páscoa / viajaram para o litoral **7** Bom dia. Estou procurando uma camisa / uma blusa verde; o que vocês têm no tamanho grande? / Qual é o preço? / Não gosto muito da cor. Tem (alguma) em azul? / Posso experimentar essa que você tem aí? / É muito grande. Não tem mais pequena? / Que pena! Obrigado/a. **8a** False **b** True **c** False **d** True **e** False **f** False **9** missing words: piscina tropical / jogar / fazer / pescar / fazer / bar **10a** Luxury apartments at country hotel **b** nature trails, waterfalls, lakes **c** coffee, juices and bread rolls **d** in the bar **e** light meals, tea and cakes, variety of national and international drinks

Portuguese–English glossary

Words and expressions appear in the glossary with the meaning they have in the context of this course; it is often the case that expressions have a variety of meanings, depending on how they are used. A good dictionary is indispensable for improving your all-round language acquisition.

abacaxi (m)	*pineapple*
aberto/a	*open*
abertura (f)	*opening (hours)*
abração (m)	*big hug*
abrir	*to open*
absurdo/a	*absurd*
acabar	*to end / finish*
acabar de ...	*to have just ...*
academia (f)	*gym*
açaí (m)	*açaí berry*
acarajé (m)	*black-eyed pea fritter*
acerola (f)	*acerola berry*
acesso (m)	*access*
achar	*to find / think*
acompanhamento (m)	*accompaniment / side dish*
aconselhar	*to advise*
acontecer	*to happen*
acreditar	*to believe*
adeus	*goodbye*
adorar	*to love / adore*
aeroporto (m)	*airport*
agora	*now*
agradável	*pleasant*
água mineral (f)	*mineral water*
aguardente (m)	*another name for **cachaça**, a sugar cane spirit similar to white rum*
ah é?	*is that so? / really?*
aí	*there / and then*
ajuda (f)	*help*

ajudar	*to help*
Alemanha (f)	*Germany*
alemão/ã	*German*
alérgico/a (a / ao)	*allergic (to)*
algodão (m)	*cotton*
alguns / algumas (mpl / fpl)	*some / any*
ali	*over there*
aliás	*what's more*
alimentação (f)	*food*
alívio	*relief;* **que alívio!** *what a relief!*
almoço (m)	*lunch*
alto/a	*tall*
aluno/a (m / f)	*school pupil*
amanhã	*tomorrow*
amarelo/a	*yellow*
ameixa (f)	*plum*
amendoim torrado (m)	*roasted peanut*
americano/a	*American*
amigo/a (m / f)	*friend*
andar	*to walk*
andar (m)	*floor*
aniversário (m)	*birthday / anniversary*
antes (de)	*before*
ao lado (de)	*next to*
ao / à / aos / às	*to the / at the*
apartamento (m)	*apartment / flat / room (in hotel)*
apertado/a	*tight*
aquele/a	*that (one)*
aqui	*here*
ar condicionado (m)	*air conditioning*
árbitro (m)	*referee*
Argentina (f)	*Argentina*
arroz doce (m)	*sweet rice / rice pudding*
assado/a	*roasted*
assim	*in this way / and so*
assinar	*to sign*
assistir	*to watch / attend*
até	*until / up to*
até amanhã	*see you tomorrow*

até de noite	*even at night*
até logo	*see you later*
até mais tarde	*see you later on*
atrações (fpl)	*attractions / entertainment*
atrás (de)	*behind*
atrasado/a	*late*
atravessar	*to cross (over)*
aula (f)	*lesson*
automóvel	*car*
avenida (f)	*avenue*
avião (m)	*aeroplane;* **por avião** *by air*
azeite (m)	*(olive) oil*
azul	*blue*
azul turquesa	*turquoise*
Baile (m) **das Debutantes**	*Debutantes' Ball*
bairro (m)	*district*
baixo/a	*short / low*
banana (f)	*banana*
banheira (f)	*bathtub*
banheiro (m)	*bathroom*
bar (m)	*bar*
barato / a	*cheap*
barba (f)	*beard*
barca (f)	*boat / ferry*
barco (m)	*boat / ferry*
barulhento/a	*noisy*
barulho (m)	*noise*
basquete (m)	*basketball*
bastante	*quite / enough*
batatas fritas (fpl)	*chips*
batida (f)	*cocktail*
batida (f) **de côco**	*coconut cocktail*
batizado (m)	*christening*
bauru (m)	*sandwich made with French bread, containing roast beef, tomatoes, pickles and melted cheese*
beber	*to drink*
bebida (f)	*drink*
bege	*beige*
beijo (m)	*kiss*

beleza!	*fantastic!*
bem	*well / well then;* **tudo bem?** *is everything OK?;* **tudo bem** *everything's OK*
bengala (f)	*walking stick*
beterraba (f)	*beetroot*
bicicleta (f)	*bicycle*
bigode (m)	*moustache*
bilhete (m)	*ticket*
biodiversidade (f)	*biodiversity*
biquíni (m)	*bikini*
blusa (f)	*blouse*
boa estada! / boa estadia!	*have a nice stay!*
boa noite	*good evening / goodnight*
boa tarde	*good afternoon / good evening*
boa viagem!	*bon voyage!*
boas férias!	*have a good holiday!*
boate (f)	*nightclub*
bolo (m) **(de limão)**	*(lemon) cake*
bolsa (f)	*bag*
bom dia	*good morning / hello*
bom / boa / bons / boas	*good*
bombom (pl **bombons**) (m)	*sweet*
bonitinho/a	*pretty / cute*
botas (fpl)	*boots*
branco/a	*white*
Brasil (m)	*Brazil*
brigar	*to argue / fight*
brincar	*to play*
cabelos (mpl)	*hair*
cachaça (f)	*sugar cane spirit similar to white rum*
cachoeira (f)	*waterfall*
cachorro (m)	*dog / hot dog*
cada	*each*
café (m)	*café / coffee*
café (m) **com leite**	*white coffee*
café (m) **da manhã**	*breakfast*
cafezinho (m)	*espresso*
caipirinha (f)	*cocktail made from cachaça, lime juice, sugar and crushed ice*
caixa (f)	*box / check out*

caixa automático (m)	*ATM / cash machine*
calça (f)	*trousers*
calçadão (m)	*promenade*
calmo/a	*calm*
cama (f)	*bed*
camarões (mpl)	*shrimps*
caminhada (f)	*walk / stroll*
caminho	*way;* **a caminho para** *on the way to*
camisa (f)	*shirt*
camiseta (f)	*T-shirt*
Canadá (m)	*Canada*
canal (m) **de televisão**	*TV channel*
canja (f)	*chicken broth*
cansado/a	*tired*
canto (m)	*corner (inside)*
cardápio (m)	*menu*
careca	*bald*
Carnaval (m)	*Carnival*
carne assada (f)	*roast meat*
carne de sol (f)	*sundried meat*
caro/a	*expensive*
carro (m)	*car*
carta (f)	*letter*
cartão (m)	*card*
carteira (f)	*wallet / purse / card*
carteira (f) **de estudante**	*student card*
carteira (f) **de identidade**	*ID card*
casa (f)	*house;* **em casa** *at home*
casado/a	*married*
casamento (m)	*wedding*
castanho/a	*brown (hair / eyes)*
castelo (m)	*castle*
catedral (f)	*cathedral*
cavalo (m)	*horse*
cê = você	*you*
cedo	*early*
cenoura (f)	*carrot*
Central (f) **de Informação Turística (CIT)**	*tourist information centre*
centro (m) **da cidade**	*city centre*

Centro (m) **de Convenções**	*conference centre*
centro (m) **financeiro e comercial**	*financial and commercial centre*
centro cultural (m)	*cultural centre*
certo	*of course / certainly / right*
cerveja (f)	*beer*
cetim (m)	*satin*
chá (m) **(com leite)**	*tea (with milk)*
chamar-se	*to be called*
chapéu (m)	*hat*
chato/a	*boring / annoying*
chegar	*to arrive*
China (f)	*China*
chope (m)	*draught beer*
churrascaria (f)	*steak house*
churrasco (m)	*barbecue*
chuveiro (m)	*shower (in bathroom)*
cidade (f)	*town / city*
cigarro (m)	*cigarette*
cima: em cima (de)	*on top (of)*
cinema (m)	*cinema*
cinto (m)	*belt*
cinza	*grey*
claro/a	*clear / light*
clube (m)	*club*
cofre (m)	*safe deposit box*
coisa (f)	*thing*
com	*with*
com certeza	*certainly*
com licença	*excuse me*
combinar	*to go with / match*
começar	*to start / begin*
comer	*to eat*
comida (baiana / mineira) (f)	*food (from Bahia / Minas)*
comida (f) **por quilo**	*food sold by weight*
complicado/a	*complicated*
compras	*shopping;* **fazer compras** *to go shopping*
comum/ns (sing / pl)	*common*
concordar	*to agree*
concurso público (m)	*civil service exam*
conhecer	*to know (person / place)*

conosco	*with us*
consultório (m)	*surgery*
conta (f)	*bill;* **por conta própria** *on one's own*
contar	*to count*
contente	*happy / content*
convenção (f)	*conference*
convencional	*standard class*
convidado (m)	*guest (at party, etc.)*
convite (m)	*invitation*
cor (f)	*colour*
coragem (f)	*courage*
cor-de-rosa	*pink*
correio (m)	*post office*
correr	*to run*
couro (m)	*leather*
coxinha (f)	*large deep-fried chicken and potato cake*
cozido/a	*boiled*
cozinha (f)	*kitchen*
cozinheiro/a (m / f)	*cook*
crianças (fpl) **(de colo)**	*children (on lap)*
cru / crua	*raw*
cruzar	*to cross*
cultura (f)	*culture*
curto/a	*short*
custar	*to cost*
daí	*and then / and so*
dançar	*to dance*
dar	*to give*
dar certo	*to turn out OK*
dar para	*to look out on*
data (f) **de nascimento**	*date of birth*
de / do / da / dos / das	*of (the) / from (the)*
debaixo (de)	*under / underneath*
decepcionado / a	*disappointed*
decidir	*to decide*
décimo/a	*tenth*
deixar	*to leave / let*
demais	*too (much)*
demorar	*to take a long time*
dentista (m / f)	*dentist*

dentro (de)	*inside / within*
depois (de)	*after / afterwards*
desaparecer	*to disappear*
descer	*to go down*
desconto (m)	*discount*
desculpe	*sorry / excuse me*
despertador (m)	*alarm clock*
destino (m)	*destination*
detestar	*to hate / detest*
Deus me livre!	*God forbid!*
devagar	*slowly*
dever	*to have to / owe*
devolver	*to return (take back)*
dia (m)	*day;* **o dia todo** *all day;* **todos os dias** *every day*
Dia (m) **da Independência**	*Independence Day*
Dia (m) **da Proclamação da República**	*Day of the Proclamation of the Republic*
diário/a	*daily*
diferente	*different*
difícil / difíceis (sing / pl)	*difficult*
dinheiro (m)	*money*
direções (fpl)	*directions*
direita	*right;* **à direita** *on / to the right*
direto/a	*straight / direct*
divertido/a	*funny / enjoyable*
divertir-se	*to enjoy oneself*
dividir	*to divide / share*
divorciado/a	*divorced*
dizer	*to say / tell*
doce	*sweet*
domingo (m)	*Sunday*
dona de casa (f)	*housewife*
durante	*during*
e	*and*
e daí?	*and so? / so what?*
e tal	*and so on / and whatever*
economia (f)	*economy / economics*
edifício (m)	*building*
ele / ela	*he / she / it*
eles / elas	*they*

eletricista (m / f)	*electrician*
eletrodomésticos (mpl)	*household appliances*
elevador (m)	*lift*
email (m)	*email*
embalagem (f)	*package*
empregada (f)	*maid*
empregado/a (m / f)	*employee / clerk*
empresa (f)	*business*
encanador/ora (m / f)	*plumber*
encontrar	*to meet / find*
endereço (m)	*address*
engarrafamento (m)	*traffic jam*
engraçado/a	*funny / amusing*
enorme	*huge*
enquanto	*while*
ensino médio (m)	*secondary school education*
então	*then / well then / in that case*
entender	*to understand*
entrada (f)	*entrance*
entregar	*to hand over / deliver*
época (f) **seca / de chuva**	*dry / rainy season*
Escócia (f)	*Scotland*
escola (f) **primária**	*primary school*
escolher	*to choose*
escrever	*to write*
escritório (m)	*office*
escuro/a	*dark*
escutar	*to listen (to)*
esfirra(f)	*Lebanese-style bread cake with minced meat filling*
Espanha (f)	*Spain*
espanhol/a	*Spanish*
especial	*special*
especialidade (f) **da casa**	*house speciality*
esperar	*to wait / hope*
esporte (m)	*sport*
esposa (f)	*wife*
esposo (m)	*husband*
esquerda	*left;* **à esquerda** *on / to the left*
esquina (f)	*corner (street)*

estação (f)	*station*
estacionamento (grátis) (m)	*(free) parking*
Estados Unidos (mpl)	*USA*
estar	*to be*
estar com calor / frio	*to be hot / cold*
estar com fome / sede	*to be hungry / thirsty*
estar com pressa	*to be in a hurry*
este / esta (m / f)	*this (one)*
estilo (m)	*style*
estrada (f)	*road*
estrelas (fpl)	*stars*
eu	*I*
evento (m)	*event*
exatamente	*exactly*
executivo	*luxury standard*
experimentar	*to try on*
explicar	*to explain*
extra grande	*extra large*
fácil	*easy;* **de fácil acesso** *easily accessible*
faculdade (f)	*faculty (university)*
falador/ora	*talkative*
falar	*to speak / talk*
falta (f) **de (educação)**	*lack of (good manners)*
faltar	*to be lacking / missing*
família (f)	*family*
fantasma (m)	*ghost*
farmácia (f)	*chemist's*
fazenda (f)	*farm / estate*
fazer	*to do / make*
fechado/a	*closed*
fechar	*to close*
feijoada (f)	*black bean stew*
feio/a	*ugly*
feira hippy (f)	*artisan market*
feirinha (f)	*marketplace*
feriado (m)	*bank holiday*
férias (fpl)	*holidays*
festa (f)	*party*
Festa (f) **de Quinze Anos**	*fifteenth birthday party*
Festas Juninas (fpl)	*'June' festivals*

ficar	*to stay / be located / become*
ficha (f)	*form*
ficha (f) **de registro de entrada no hotel**	*hotel check-in form*
filho/a (m / f)	*son / daughter*
fim (m)	*end*
fim (m) **de semana**	*weekend;* **no fim de semana** *at the weekend*
florido/a	*flowery*
foto (f)	*photo*
França (f)	*France*
frente	*front;* **em frente (de)** *in front (of) / opposite*
frigobar (m)	*minibar*
frio/a	*cold*
frito/a	*fried*
fruta (f)	*fruit*
fumar	*to smoke*
funcionar	*to function / work*
funcionário público (m)	*civil servant*
fusos horários (mpl)	*time zones*
futebol (m)	*football*
galera (f)	*folks, guys;* **oi galera!** *hi guys! / hi folks!*
ganhar	*to win*
garagem (f)	*garage*
garçom (m)	*waiter*
garfo (m)	*fork*
garrafa (f)	*bottle*
gás (m)	*gas;* **com / sem gás** *fizzy / still (drinks)*
gastar	*to spend*
gato (m)	*cat*
geada (f)	*frost*
gelo (m)	*ice;* **com / sem gelo** *with / without ice*
gengibre (m)	*ginger*
Gente!	*You guys!*
gentil/is (sing / pl)	*kind*
geralmente	*generally*
gerente (m / f)	*manager*
gordo/a	*fat*
gorjeta (f)	*tip*
gostar (de)	*to like*
gostoso/a	*tasty / nice*

grande	*large / big*
gravata (f)	*tie*
grego/a	*Greek*
grelhado/a	*grilled*
grisalho/a	*grey (hair)*
guaraná (m)	*refreshing fizzy drink made with the Amazonian fruit of the same name*
há	*there is / are*
hambúrguer (m)	*hamburger*
havaianas (fpl)	*flip-flops*
hoje	*today*
homem (pl **homens**) (m)	*man*
hora (f)	*hour / time;* **a qualquer hora** *at any time*
horário (m)	*timetable*
horrível	*horrible*
hortelã (f)	*mint*
hóspede (m)	*guest*
hospital (pl **hospitais**) (m)	*hospital*
hotel (pl **hotéis**) (m)	*hotel*
hotel-fazenda (m)	*country hotel*
ida: de ida	*single;* **de ida e volta** *return*
idoso/a	*old / aged*
igreja (f)	*church*
ilha (f)	*island*
importar-se	*to mind*
incomodar	*to disturb / bother*
indicar	*to indicate / show*
Inglaterra (f)	*England*
inglês/a	*English*
ingresso (m)	*entrance ticket*
inteirinho/a	*complete / whole*
inteligente	*clever*
interessar	*to interest*
interior (m)	*interior (inland)*
inverno (m)	*winter*
ir	*to go*
irmão/ã (m / f)	*brother / sister*
italiano/a	*Italian*
já	*already / now*
já que ...	*(seeing) as ...*

janela (f)	*window*
jantar (fora)	*to dine (out)*
jaqueta (f)	*jacket*
jardim (pl **jardins**) (m)	*garden*
jeans (mpl)	*jeans*
jeito	*way;* **ter jeito** *to work out OK / to be possible*
jogar	*to play (sport)*
jogo (m)	*game / match*
jornal (pl **jornais**) (m)	*newspaper*
juros	*interest;* **sem juros** *without interest*
lá	*there*
lã (f)	*wool*
ladrão (m)	*thief*
lago (m)	*lake*
lanche (m)	*snack*
lanchonete (m)	*snack bar / café*
laranja (f)	*orange*
lazer (m)	*leisure*
legal!	*brilliant! / great!*
lembrança (f)	*souvenir*
lençól (pl **lençóis**) (m)	*sheet*
lentes (fpl) **de contato**	*contact lenses*
ler	*to read*
levantar peso	*to weight-lift*
levantar-se	*to get up*
levar	*to take*
leve	*light (in weight)*
limpar	*to clean*
limpo/a	*clean*
linguiça (f)	*pork sausage*
linha (f)	*line / platform*
linho (m)	*linen*
liquidação (f)	*sale*
listrado/a	*striped*
litoral (m)	*coast*
livraria (f)	*bookshop*
livrinho (m) **de informações**	*information booklet*
local (m) **de nascimento**	*place of birth*
loiro/a	*blonde*
loja (f)	*shop*

loja (f) **de departamentos**	*department store*
longe	*far (off)*
longo/a	*long*
lugar (m)	*place*
luxuoso/a	*luxury*
maçã (f)	*apple*
mãe (f)	*mother*
maiô (m)	*swimsuit*
maior	*larger / greater*
mais	*more*
mais ou menos	*more or less*
mal	*badly*
mala (f)	*suitcase*
mandar	*to send*
mandioca frita (f)	*fried cassava*
manga (f) **comprida / curta**	*long / short sleeved*
manhã (f)	*morning;* **da / de manhã** *in the morning;* **de manhã cedo** *early in the morning*
mão (f)	*hand;* **boa mão** *'good hand' (refers to a good cook);* **má mão** *'bad hand' (refers to a bad cook)*
mapa (m)	*map / plan*
maracujá (m)	*passion fruit*
marido (m)	*husband*
marrom	*brown*
mas	*but*
mau / má / maus / más	*bad*
máximo/a	*best*
médico/a (m / f)	*doctor*
médio/a	*medium*
meia-noite (f)	*midnight*
meias (fpl)	*socks*
meio-dia (m)	*midday*
melhor	*better / best*
menor	*smaller*
menos	*less*
mensagem (f)	*message*
mercado (m)	*market*
mergulhar	*to dive*
metrô (m)	*underground*

meu Deus!	*goodness me!*
meu/s (m / pl)	*my*
mil	*(a) thousand*
minha/s (f / pl)	*my*
moça (f)	*girl*
moda (f)	*fashion;* **na moda** *in fashion*
molho (m)	*sauce;* **molho de churrasco / vinagrete / agridoce** *barbecue sauce / vinaigrette / sweet and sour sauce*
momento (m)	*moment*
montanha russa (f)	*rollercoaster*
montão	*pile;* **um montão de ...** *a pile of ...*
monte (m)	*hill*
morango (m)	*strawberry*
morar	*to live*
moreno/a	*brown / tanned*
mostrar	*to show*
motorista (m / f)	*driver*
mousse (m)	*mousse*
móveis (mpl)	*furniture*
movimentado/a	*busy (place)*
mudar	*to change*
muitas vezes (fpl)	*many times / often*
muito/a/os/as	*much / many*
muito prazer	*pleased to meet you*
mulher (f)	*wife / woman*
mundo (m)	*world*
museu (m)	*museum*
música (f) **(sertaneja)**	*(country) music*
nada	*nothing*
nadar	*to swim*
namorado/a (m / f)	*boy / girlfriend*
não	*no, not*
não sei	*I don't know*
naquele / naquela / naqueles / naquelas	*in that / those, on that / those*
Natal (m)	*Christmas*
né?	*isn't it? / aren't you? etc.*
negócio (m)	*business*
neste / nesta / nestes / nestas	*in this / these, on this / these*

neve (f)	*snow*
noite (f)	*night;* **da / de noite** *at night*
nome (m)	*name*
nono/a	*ninth*
normalmente	*normally*
nós	*we*
nossa!	*wow!*
nosso/a/s (m / f / pl)	*our*
notícias (fpl)	*news*
novela (f)	*soap opera*
novo/a	*new / young;* **de novo** *again*
número (m) **de identidade / passaporte**	*ID / passport number*
nunca	*never*
nuvem (pl **nuvens**) (f)	*cloud*
obrigado/a	*thank you*
óculos (mpl)	*glasses*
odear	*to hate*
oferta (f)	*offer;* **na oferta** *on offer*
oi!	*hi!*
oitavo/a	*eighth*
olhar	*to look*
olhos (mpl)	*eyes*
onde?	*where?*
ônibus (m)	*bus;* **ônibus leito** *sleeper bus (with reclining seats)*
ontem	*yesterday*
ótimo!	*great! / brilliant!*
ótimo/a	*great / best*
ou	*or*
outra vez (f)	*again*
ouvir	*to hear / listen to*
ovo (m)	*egg*
ovos recheados (mpl)	*stuffed eggs*
padaria (f)	*bakery*
pagar	*to pay*
pai (m)	*father*
país (m)	*country*
paisagem (f)	*countryside*
palmito (m)	*heart of palm*
pão (m)	*bread*

papel (pl **papéis**) (m)	*paper*
par (m)	*pair*
para	*for / to / in order to*
para mim	*for me*
parabéns!	*congratulations!*
parada (f)	*stop (bus)*
parecer	*to seem*
parede (f)	*wall (of building)*
parque (m)	*park*
partir	*to leave / break;* **a partir de** *… from … (time)*
Páscoa (f)	*Easter*
passagem (f)	*ticket (for travel)*
passar	*to pass / spend (time)*
pavê (m) **de abacaxi**	*creamy biscuit tart with pineapple*
pé (m)	*foot*
peça (f)	*piece*
pechincha!	*bargain!*
pedaço (m)	*bit / piece*
pedir	*to ask (for)*
pegar	*to get / grab / catch*
peixe (m)	*fish*
pena	*pity;* **que pena!** *what a shame / pity!*
pensar	*to think*
pequeno/a	*small*
perder	*to lose*
perfumaria (f)	*perfume shop / perfume counter*
pergunta (f)	*question*
perguntar	*to ask (question)*
pertinho	*really close*
perto	*near / close*
pescar	*to fish*
pesquisa (f)	*survey*
péssimo / a	*awful*
pessoas (fpl)	*people*
pessoas com deficiência	*disabled people*
pessoas com mobilidade reduzida	*people with reduced mobility*
picanha (f) **com feijão**	*rump steak with black beans*
picante	*spicy*
pimenta (m)	*pepper (spice)*

pinga (f)	*another name for* **cachaça**, *a sugar cane spirit similar to white rum*
pipoca (f)	*popcorn*
piscina (f)	*swimming pool*
plataforma (f)	*platform*
poder	*to be able / know how to*
pois não?	*can I help you?*
política (f)	*politics*
poluído/a	*polluted*
ponto (m) **de ônibus**	*bus stop*
por	*per*
por avião / estrada	*by air / road*
por conta própria	*on one's own*
por mês / semana / ano	*per month / week / year*
porção (f)	*portion*
porcaria (f)	*mess / shambles*
porco (m) **grelhado**	*grilled pork*
porque	*because*
porta (f)	*door*
portão (m)	*gate*
porto (m)	*port*
Portugal	*Portugal*
possível	*possible*
poucas vezes (fpl)	*not often / seldom*
pousada (f)	*hotel*
praça (f)	*square (town)*
praça (f) **da alimentação**	*food hall*
praia (f)	*beach*
prato (m)	*plate / dish*
prato principal (m)	*main course*
prazo	*time limit;* **à prazo** *in instalments*
precisar	*to need*
preço (m)	*price*
prédio (m) **de apartamentos**	*block of flats*
preencher	*to fill in (form)*
preferir	*to prefer*
pregado/a	*worn out / tired*
presente (m)	*present / gift*
presunto (m)	*ham*
preto/a	*black*

previsto/a	*forecast / expected*
primeiro/a	*first*
primo/a (m / f)	*cousin*
prioridade (f)	*priority*
pro / pra (= para o / a)	*for the*
procura	*search;* **à procura de** *looking for / on the lookout for*
produtos (mpl) **de limpeza**	*cleaning products*
professor / ora (m / f)	*teacher*
proibido fumar	*no smoking*
promoção (f)	*promotion* (sale); **em promoção** *on special offer*
pronto!	*there!*
provador (m)	*changing room*
provar	*to try*
próximo/a	*next*
qual?	*what / which?*
quantos? / quantas? (mpl / fpl)	*how many?*
quarta-feira (f)	*Wednesday*
quarteirão (m)	*block (street)*
quarto (m)	*(bed)room*
quarto (m) **de casal**	*double room*
quarto (m) **de solteiro**	*single room*
quarto (m) **para família**	*family room*
quarto/a	*fourth*
quase nunca	*almost never / hardly ever*
que	*that / which / who*
que lindo / a!	*how pretty / lovely!*
que sorte!	*what good luck!*
que tal …?	*how about / what about …?*
queijo (m)	*cheese*
quente	*hot*
querer	*to want / wish*
quinta-feira (f)	*Thursday*
quinto / a	*fifth*
rádio (m)	*radio*
rapidinho	*really quick*
raramente	*rarely*
razão (f)	*reason*
real (m) (pl **reis**)	*real (currency)*

realmente	*really*
receita (f)	*recipe*
recepção (f)	*reception*
recepcionista (mf)	*receptionist*
recheado/a	*filled / stuffed*
recomendar	*to recommend*
refeição (pl **refeições**) (f)	*meal*
refeição (f) **ligeira**	*light meal*
relaxante	*relaxing*
relaxar	*to relax*
relógio (m)	*clock / watch*
repetir	*to repeat*
reportagem (f)	*report*
reserva (f)	*reservation / (nature) reserve*
responder	*to reply*
restaurante (m)	*restaurant*
reunião (f)	*meeting*
Reveillon (m)	*New Year's Eve*
rio (m)	*river*
ritmo (m)	*rhythm*
rodeado/a por	*surrounded by*
rodoviária (f)	*bus station*
rosa (f)	*rose / pink*
roupas (fpl)	*clothes*
roxo/a	*purple*
rua (f)	*street / road*
ruim	*awful*
ruivo / a	*red-haired*
sábado (m)	*Saturday*
saber	*to know (a fact / how to do something)*
saia (f)	*skirt*
saída (f) **de emergência**	*emergency exit*
sair	*to go out*
sal (m)	*salt*
sala (f) **(de reuniões)**	*(meeting) room*
salada (f)	*salad*
saladinha (f)	*small salad*
salão (m) **de festa**	*party room*
sandálias (fpl)	*sandals*
sanduíche (m)	*sandwich*

sapatos (mpl)	shoes
saudade (f)	feeling of missing someone or something
saúde (f)	health
saúde!	cheers!
secretário/a (m / f)	secretary
seda (f)	silk
seguir	to follow / carry on
segunda-feira (f)	Monday
segundo / a	second
selva (f)	jungle
semana (f)	week
semana passada (f)	last week
Semana Santa (f)	Holy Week
sempre	always
sentir-se	to feel
separado/a	separated
ser	to be
servir (-se)	to serve (yourself)
sétimo / a	seventh
seu/s (m / pl)	his / her / its / your
sexta-feira (f)	Friday
sexto/a	sixth
shopping (m)	shopping centre
short (m)	shorts
show (m) **de música**	music show
sim	yes
sinal (m) **de trânsito**	traffic lights
sinceramente	sincerely / truthfully
só	only / just
sobre	about
sobremesa (f)	dessert
sobrenome (m)	surname
sobrinho/a (m / f)	nephew / niece
solteiro/a	single
som/ns (m / pl)	sound / s
sombra (f)	shade; **na sombra** in the shade
sorvete (m)	ice cream
sua/s (f / pl)	his / her / its / your
subir	to go up / climb
subsolo (m)**: no subsolo**	underground

suco (m)	*juice*
sugerir	*to suggest*
sujo/a	*dirty*
sunga (f)	*swimming trunks*
super-...	*really*
super-bonito/a	*really good-looking*
supermercado (m)	*supermarket*
suportar	*to put up with*
tá?	*OK?*
talvez	*perhaps*
tamanho (m)	*size*
tão	*so*
tarde	*afternoon / evening;* **da / de tarde** *in the afternoon / evening*
tchau	*bye*
tchin tchin!	*cheers!*
teatro (m)	*theatre*
telefonar	*to telephone*
tempão (m)	*long time*
tempo (m)	*weather / time*
tênis (m / mpl)	*tennis / trainers*
ter	*to have*
ter jeito	*to work out / be convenient*
terça-feira (f)	*Tuesday*
terceiro/a	*third*
terminar	*to end / finish*
terno (m)	*men's suit*
tio/a (m / f)	*uncle / aunt*
tipo (m)	*type / sort*
tirar	*to take / take out*
tô (= estou)	*I'm*
toalha (f)	*towel*
tocar	*to touch / play (instrument)*
tomar	*to have (food, drink) / take (medicine)*
torneira (f)	*tap*
torpedo (m)	*message*
torrada (f)	*toast*
trabalhar	*to work*
trabalho (m)	*work*
tranquilo / a	*calm*

travesseiro (m)	*pillow*
trazer	*to bring*
trem (pl trens) (m)	*train*
trilha (f)	*trail*
triste	*sad*
troco (m)	*change (money)*
turismo (m) **de aventura**	*adventure tourism*
último/a	*last*
um pouco	*a little (bit)*
universidade (f)	*university*
usar	*to use / wear*
uso (m) **exclusivo**	*exclusive use*
vale a pena	*it's worth it*
valeu!	*good stuff! / you bet! / appreciated!*
variedade (f)	*variety*
vatapá (m)	*shrimp curry*
veludo (m)	*velvet*
vender	*to sell*
ventilador (m)	*fan*
ver	*to see*
verão (m)	*summer*
verdade!	*true! / correct!*
verde	*green*
vermelho / a	*red*
vestido (m)	*dress*
vestir-se	*to get dressed*
vez (f)	*time;* **uma vez** *once*
viagem (pl viagens) (f)	*journey*
viajar	*to travel*
vinagre (m)	*vinegar*
vinho (m)	*wine*
vinho (m) **da casa**	*house wine*
vinho (m) **tinto / branco**	*red / white wine*
vir	*to come*
virar	*to turn*
visita (f)	*visit*
visitante (m)	*visitor*
visitar	*to visit*
vista (f)	*view;* **à vista** *in cash*
vitrine (f)	*shop window*

viúvo/a (m / f)	*widower / widow*
vizinhos (mpl)	*neighbours*
você/s	*you*
vôlei (m)	*volleyball*
voltar	*to return*
vontade	*will;* **à vontade** *at will*
vôo (m)	*flight*
xadrez (m)	*chess*
x-búrguer (m)	*cheeseburger*
xícara (f) **de café**	*cup of coffee*
xinxim (m) **de galinha**	*spicy chicken stew*